O LOVE THAT WILL NOT LET ME GO

DAVID ALDOUS

LONDON ● COLORADO SPRINGS ● HYDERABAD

O LOVE THAT WILL NOT LET ME GO

'It's one thing to believe in the love of God, but quite another to know its transforming power. In this personal and honest account David unpacks how this love feels and what this love does. It's a tonic for those of us who sometimes forget just how broad and deep this love really is.'
Revd Dr Rob Frost, Director of Share Jesus International

'In a world of brokenness and pain, a world that I spend most of my time in here in Baghdad, we need to know a "love that will not let us go". That love of Jesus that journeys with us is the only thing that truly offers us hope. David Aldous shares with us his unique journey of love. In this book you too can come on this same journey and find above all the loving father heart of God.'
Canon Andrew White, President of the FRRME & Vicar of Baghdad

'David Aldous's *O Love That Will Not Let Me Go* is as honest, down to earth, and good humoured as the man himself. Taken right out of the pages of his real life journal, David lets us live inside his heart and head as he searches to have that deep calling answered. We find him finding the satisfying love and true friendship of God revealed and experienced in the day-to-day events of everyman's life. *O Love That Will Not Let Me Go* will get hold of you with a voice you recognise already, but maybe are not realising, and it will not let you go until the love of the One who is speaking has embraced you with both arms. It's so easy to just hug back!

Thanks, David, for helping us to open the arms of our lives to the One who has captured our hearts!'
Mahesh and Bonnie Chavda, Mahesh Chavda Ministries, USA

'His love is the greatest gift God has given to mankind and, apart from the Bible, the greatest understanding of that love is spoken in testimony. Thank you, thank you David for yours!'
Paul Jones, presenter and lead singer with The Manfreds

'David's book, *O Love That Will Love Not Me Go* is a moving personal testimony of God's awesome love and perfect concern for his children. It is a powerful personal journey into the very heart of Father God. As you read, you will be moved to a warmer, securer place in God, finding you, too, are his very own special child and he will do anything for you.'
Dr Heidi Gail Baker, Founding Director of Iris Ministries

13 12 11 10 09 08 07   7 6 5 4 3 2 1

First published 2007 by Authentic Media
9 Holdom Avenue, Bletchley, Milton Keynes, Bucks, MK1 1QR, UK
1820 Jet Stream Drive, Colorado Springs, CO 80921, USA
OM Authentic Media, Medchal Road, Jeedimetla Village,
Secunderabad 500 055, A.P., India
www.authenticmedia.co.uk

Authentic Media is a division of IBS-STL UK, a company limited by guarantee
(registered charity no. 270162)

British Library Cataloguing in Publication Data
A catalogue record for this book is available from the British Library

ISBN: 978-1-86024-610-4

Cover Design by fourninezero design.
Print Management by Adare Carwin
Printed and bound in Great Britain by J.H. Haynes & Co., Sparkford

For Jane, Tash, Kim
Jems and Lou

.

CONTENTS

FOREWORD
BY DON HEGINBOTHAM

It was with some apprehension that I responded when asked to review the manuscript of David Aldous's first book, *O Love That Will Not Let Me Go*; I had not realised that David was even considering writing a book. So imagine my surprise when on the very first page I was drawn in and embraced by David's candour, humour and heart-wrenching vulnerability.

David is a man of many parts and has a wide variety of life experiences to draw on: driving a London bus while 'resting' as an actor, teaching Drama, English and Religious Education at a comprehensive school, spinning the discs as a jock during the heady days of the eighties, and currently presenting television and radio programmes.

It is with this background that David begins a journey of self-discovery asking the age old questions of life and love, and does God really care for a world that is in disarray with wars, hurt and suffering; in this quest comes the still, quiet voice of God with 'a love that will not let him go'.

This book challenges the complacency of the present day church with its lip service to the love of God and the needs of others, and gently provokes the unbeliever to consider the claims of the 'Man From Nazareth'.

Don Heginbotham
Producer, God TV

FOREWORD
BY JOHN PANTRY

At certain times in every Christian's life there are moments when the world around seems to fade into the distance and the wonderful presence of God becomes overwhelming. It was at such a moment 'When the things of earth become strangely dim' that David heard our Father remind him of His unconditional love. It heralded a period of 7 days that were to change David's understanding and bring him closer to God than ever.

Here at Premier Radio, we've got used to seeing David in his motorbike gear striding into the office, all tangled hair, wild beard and leathers, larger than life and twice as loud! However, it's becoming clear that God is doing a deep work in his life, bringing a new depth and softness. David has always been a single-minded and passionate man who throws himself wholeheartedly into whatever he's doing and it's his prayer that this book will reveal some of the open secrets to engaging with the living God. Like so many extroverts, David's booming voice and bravado are a shield for a sensitive soul that seems able to place its trust in God alone.

However, unusually for an Englishman, a few moments spent with him will reveal that he's an open book, a man without guile or airs and graces – brutally honest about his own faults, gentle and forgiving of others. Knowing that we are loved unconditionally is knowledge that is healing, life-giving and confidence-building. It's done wonders for David. I pray that you'll soak up something of the nature of God as you read David's story and one day in the vast expanses of heaven you'll seek David out and rejoice together in the knowledge of God's unconditional love.

John Pantry
Premier Radio

ACKNOWLEDGEMENTS

My great appreciation goes firstly to my dear friend and brother in Christ, Edward John, for all his encouragement in the working of this project. For his obedience in passing on the Lord's prophetic words. For suggesting in the first place to write this book.

My love and gratitude go to Patricia Taylor-Shipley for all the hard work in editing my first book – what a mammoth task that was. I didn't expect the editing to begin after the sixth word, however. It just goes to show that my grammar leaves a lot to be desired.

Thanks to Malcolm Down and the team at Authentic Media for the hard work in producing this book. Thank you so much for your kind words of encouragement and faith in this whole project. You are without doubt world-beaters at what you do.

My grateful thanks go to my producer Don Heginbotham for the words of support whilst writing this book. For politely laughing in all the right places and crying when was necessary. Bless you Don and your wife Heather.

My love and grateful thanks go to my family for allowing me the time and space to be able to write, and for reading and rereading the manuscript, for the kind suggestions, the thoughtful criticism, and for allowing me to write their story too.

Finally, my thanks to my Lord Jesus Christ, for inspiring me to write this book. I never ever thought I would be able to do it. Thank you Jesus for this wonderful gift.

INTRODUCTION

PERFECT LOVE DRIVES OUT FEAR

I was being propelled along the M25 by my motorbike, on my way home after a rather interesting conference in London. I had been praying most of the way there and all of the way back. 'What were you praying about?' I hear you ask. Well I'm glad you asked me that. I was in deep intercession due to a comment a friend of mine had made about this book you are about to read. Back then it was merely in manuscript form. He told me some things that made me really think. He explained that if I wanted to write a book about love, then this 'masterpiece' must contain certain elements, some of which I had omitted. I was deeply troubled by these comments and wanted to check with God as to what He thought. Had I done wrong in not mentioning certain things? I seemed to wait an eternity for an answer from the Lord and I was wondering why. Suddenly, the Lord spoke to me.

'David, this work is about My love for you, My love for My people.'

This made perfect sense to me. My heavenly Father had told me before during a similar journey to, 'Tell My people about My love'. Why had I forgotten? Why hadn't I remembered that?

Hang on, where was I? I found myself speeding way past the junction I needed, by at least 9 miles. How could I have missed the turn? To my knowledge, there are three roadside signs warning about the exit, not to mention the hatch marks, and here I was way past the turn-off. I began to get very irritated with myself. *How could you have been so stupid, David? Just not concentrating again, David.* Really berating myself. I said out loud to God: 'Why Lord? Why didn't I see the junction?' Immediately I felt the reply come back to me.

'Because David, if you had turned off, then you would have had an accident.'

I couldn't believe what I had just heard. That was amazing. Incredible. I saw no signs at all, I sailed past my exit and went a further 9 miles before I had realised. The Lord had saved me from having an accident on my motorbike. 'Thank You, Father.' I mouthed to Him. 'Thank You once again for demonstrating Your love for me.'

As you read this book, you will begin to experience the journey I have been on, with God revealing to me His awesome love. What you are about to read took place over a 7-day period when I wasn't in the place I should have been. You will discover how God broke through into my life, to reveal His Son in a new and powerful way. I pray that as you read these pages, the Holy Spirit will impact your life and shine a torch on areas that need to be brought into the light, so His love can shine through and penetrate your spirit with a new clarity.

May His peace be upon you now and always.

David Aldous
30 November 2006

CHAPTER 1

SEE, I AM DOING
A NEW THING!

In my journey of self-discovery I have learned many things. Some of which I wish to share with you to help you in the journey you will make from today. My precious friend, this is a monumental day in your life. A day when you will begin to notice things that were not apparent before.

I remember when I discovered that I had a passion to understand the love of God and to get to grips with the Father heart of God; to understand how God's heart 'beats' for me. Whenever I was asked to preach or talk in Christian gatherings, I would always want to talk about God's love. If I was asked to preach on a certain subject or text from the Bible, I would try to bring God's love into the message somehow. When I reflect on that now, I understand that God's love must be in everything we try to achieve in this life. Even down to the Sunday morning preach in church. If I was given 'free rein' to preach on whatever I wanted in church, I would always, without fail, want to talk on God's love for us and how we should love Him in return.

Imagine, gentle reader, my surprise and concern, when appearing on a Christian TV station with some people I knew well and trusted absolutely, a prophetic word was spoken right into my life. This word was brought by my close friend and brother in Christ, Edward John, who out of the blue, after praying for an 'awesome' programme in the Lord, began first to speak in tongues and then BANG, brought a prophetic word. Let me now try to convey where I was in the scheme of things at that point, where I was in God at that moment. It's fairly easy actually, as I was struggling somewhat.

Nothing I had been trying to achieve seemed to be working out. I had been involved in various projects that seemed to me to go absolutely nowhere. I was feeling very rejected in a strange sort of way. Quite honestly, I was undiscovered, undernourished in God's word, unhappy, unmotivated and unbelievably fed up with everything. I remember I had on one occasion asked God to take me home. 'There is nothing for me here Lord,' I said in a moment of desperation that day. 'In everything I try to achieve I get nowhere at all. I don't feel fulfilled anymore. Where is Your love in this Father?' I cried in frustration. Yet on the face of it, I had everything that anyone would want: a successful wife, four wonderful children, four grandchildren, two dogs, a house in Essex, a second property in France, a car, and a motorbike. What more could I ever wish for?

On this particular day this was where I was. Three nasty brown envelopes had plopped onto the mat that morning, begging to be sorted out. *No I'm not dealing with that today*, I thought. Yet another problem that needed to be dealt with. 'Lord, why don't You tell me where we are going wrong here? Why can't we keep our heads above water?'

CHAPTER 2

AND SURELY I AM WITH YOU ALWAYS, TO THE VERY END OF THE AGE

It was in this sort of place, desperate, at the end of my tether, that I found myself racing up to the North of England one Saturday night for a live TV broadcast, straight after a live radio broadcast that lasted, may I just point out, for 2 hours. I was driving rather too fast as I needed to be there for 8 p.m. and was in no mood to suffer fools gladly. I duly arrived safe and sound at about 8:15 p.m., though extremely harassed, to be greeted by all and sundry saying all the things Christians usually proclaim to each other on meeting, 'Praise God how wonderful to see you,' or, 'My, my, you look well! Give me a hug.' I'm afraid on this particular evening none of this cut it with me. Someone said, 'Good evening David.'

'Is it?' I retorted.

'Get yourself ready. You will be on air very shortly. Go into the green room and just relax until we call you.' So I did. I sat, and sat, and sat. Got up. Walked around a little. Sat some more. Edward John came in.

'Hallelujah David! Good to see you. When did you get in?'

'About an hour ago,' I replied, trying to keep massive frustration and anger out of my voice. Please, gentle reader, at this point check out the language he was using compared to my inner turmoil. Notice how un-peaceful I was.

I don't know how I can do this tonight, Lord. I'm not in a good place with You at the moment. Please – give me a break here, I thought to myself.

A well-known pastor was also sitting in the green room with me, waxing lyrical about this and that, talking about his flight down, how the Lord was blessing him, what a message he had tonight, and so on and so forth. Was it making me feel more peaceful? I think not!

Well have you guessed yet? I was not asked to appear on the programme this particular night at all. All that travel, to no avail. What a complete and utter waste of my time to be driving like a complete idiot only to be rejected at the last furlong.

I wonder what sort of hotel I've been checked into. Probably a B&B somewhere nearby. Oh mercy noooo! I need some peace.

'Don,' I asked my faithful producer. 'Where am I checked in this evening?' expecting him to say the local B&B. (I was about to begin a long prolonged argument as to why I deserved better than this.) But why should I have had better than this? Who was I? No one that's who!

'You're checked into a nice hotel overlooking the sea tonight and for the next 4 days, David.'

Oh bliss! How wonderful, I can't wait. Things are looking up already.

As I reflect on this, I was beginning to realise that you can't get away with sin in your life, this anger and frustration, for too long, before it all catches up with you. You realise that you are fighting a battle that you just don't want to fight anymore. It's a confrontation with yourself, that if you are saved by the grace of our Lord Jesus Christ, you shouldn't be fighting. But I was still fighting – no doubt about it, I just longed for that peace that passes all understanding to reside in the very depths of my heart.

I don't know if you are anything like me, but some times when you are in church and waiting on God, and He doesn't show up, you think that it's Him who has departed, or didn't turn up. We never think that *we* are the ones to have gone away from *Him*. Oh no, it's never our fault is it!

Anyway, back to the story. I took Edward and another guy called Simon to the hotel that night as they were staying in the same place as me.

'David, ask for a large room and see what happens,' Simon said.

OK, I thought to myself, *here goes.*

'And can I have a large room please?' I asked the nervous-looking receptionist waiting at the counter for me to sign the registration forms.

'Certainly sir,' she replied, making me feel a sense of self-importance once again.

'Your room is number 131 on the ground floor. Along the corridor to the left, to the end, through the double doors, right and right again, down the long corridor and you are on the right hand side at the end.' There you go then, miles from anywhere, in probably the smallest room the hotel has, smaller than the broom closet.

I found my room eventually, tried to open the door with my key card, only to find the red light constantly flashing. I tried the card in a variety of different ways, getting more frustrated by the second. The fact that I was juggling three bags and my laptop while enjoying a disco light show on my hotel door, didn't help at all. 'How many ways can this card go in?' I mumbled to myself, the frustration setting off an explosion inside my head. I finally opened the door after an eternity, to reveal – a large, spacious room with a huge, comfortable bed and a well-proportioned bathroom. How fantastic! My mood changed straight away. Oh how I had been blessed!

Chapter 3

Take Heart, Son; Your Sins Are Forgiven

After a good night's sleep, I awoke to face a new day. 'What will this one hold?' I questioned myself. *Remember, it is Sunday, the Lord's day. I am supposed to go to church. Sorry Lord, I ain't in the mood for that.*

When I saw Simon at breakfast, he was about to leave. He asked me if I would like him to stay.

No actually, I would rather eat breakfast and read my paper alone.

'Of course, Simon, do join me.' See I couldn't even say what's really on my mind to people, just in case I hurt their feelings.

'I'm going into town later on, David, would you like to come?' I noticed the weather for the first time this morning. It looked extremely grey and overcast. Cold too. And when Simon had asked that question, I was thinking to myself that I had forgotten to bring a coat with me.

'Do you think that the shops will be open this morning?' I asked nonchalantly.

'I'm sure they will be.'

'Then let's go. I need to buy a coat as I don't have one.'

In no time at all we were on our way to the local town, where I quickly found a parking place. We went into the first shop we came to and I found a rather nice red coat that would do the job perfectly. I was about to make my purchase when Simon suggested that perhaps I should shop around a little, to make sure I was happy with this coat. I don't know if you are like me in this respect, but I always shop very quickly. I see something I want to buy, I buy it. I don't shop around. I don't like shopping at the best of times. You should see me Christmas shopping. Boy oh boy. I make a list of exactly what I want, and then I'm off like a whirling dervish, around the shops in no time at all. So me shopping around for a coat, isn't me at all. Trust me.

We must have gone to every single shop in this local town, without exception. Shop after shop, looking at coat after coat. *Oh deep joy*, I thought to myself.

'D'you know what, Simon?' I sighed, after what seemed to be an eternity. 'I'm going to buy the red coat I saw earlier.'

Back to the very first shop we traipse, and I made my purchase.

'Don't you feel better now that you have shopped around for that coat, David?'

Not at all. 'Absolutely Simon, what a great plan of yours!' *Back to the hotel for me for some sustenance and peace.*

For some reason when I got in the car to drive back to the studio that evening for another live telecast (that I wasn't expecting to be a part of), once again I wasn't in a great mood! I wonder why? Simon was sitting beside me and Edward was behind me in the back of the car. And guess, just guess what he was saying? Yep, you guessed it. He was praising God, praying, thanking God for what was about to happen. Suddenly he shouts, 'WHOA!' at the top of his voice, places his hands on my back and begins to prophesy over my life.

If you don't know what is meant by 'prophesying' or 'bringing a word of prophecy', quite simply, it means that someone is declaring verbally, something the Lord has put on their heart concerning you and your life. So imagine my surprise at having the Lord talk to me in this way, particularly while I was driving:

Fasten your seat belts. Sit back and just relax. What I spoke to your heart 15 years ago I am about to release unto you. Don't worry or think about how it's going to happen.

I will send the people your way. I will open up the American market – just like I promised. I'll also begin to send you workers. You've wondered why it doesn't happen. 'Why doesn't it go the way that I had thought – like it does for others?'

The Lord says, 'I will send you workers, who are hearers and doers – no more, just a little here and there! These workers will stand by you and bring you into My promise for you. I spoke to you specifically 15 years ago – dig it up! It is time now!' says the Lord.

These words shocked me. I was completely nonplussed. The tears began to flow in torrents, veritable rivers. Remember, I was trying to drive at the time. I am completely certain of one thing, that it was the Lord who drove us to the studio that evening, without a doubt. I was incapable. I was a mess. The tears were flowing thick and fast but then an overwhelming sense of peace hit my heart. I can only describe it as being awesome. I felt released across my whole being. I was being reborn right there and then. Something new was happening to me. As I write this, the tears are welling up in my eyes as I recall this significant moment in my life. (I'm on a plane flying back from Oslo at this moment and am getting some strange glances from the woman to my right.) It is such a difficult job to describe this peace. I know you will experience this for yourself during the journey you have now started.

That evening was truly awesome for all concerned. Yes! I made an appearance, and brought a word about 'giving' that was from the very throne room of grace. What a night. What an experience. What joy!

CHAPTER 4

THE LIGHT SHINES
IN THE DARKNESS,
BUT THE DARKNESS
HAS NOT UNDERSTOOD IT

I had a wonderful night's sleep that night. As I lay in bed, in my sumptuous king size, I couldn't help but reflect on God's almighty blessings. I began to drift back. The years fell away in a flash.

The year is 1975. My then wife and I are travelling to France to see her parents. They live in eastern France, a place called Annemasse, near the Swiss border. It is half past one in the morning on the 20 December. We are on a large passenger ferry travelling from Dover to Calais and are nearing the dock of Calais itself. We have with us our daughter Natasha who is just a year old. Bless her little heart, she is asleep on the back seat in her carrycot. We are in the car waiting with all the other people to disembark the ship.

'Oh look,' says Jo my wife. 'The car in front has started hiiiis engine, it's about time we did, too. I am so excited to be going home to see Maman and Papa after all thiiiis time.' (Note the alluring French accent.)

Jo hadn't seen her parents for around 12 months and we had both felt it was important to spend Christmas with them.

I digress.

I turn the key to the old Vauxhall van. Cough cough splutter splutter. Oops. The van isn't working. 'Ummm, OK, let's try again.' Whine whine cough cough sputter, clunk, spppppptttttttt.

'It won't work,' pipes up Jo.

'Oh really!' I declare, trying to keep the annoyance from my now seriously irritated voice.

I think to myself: *OK David, let's try it again and keep calm.*

Whine splutter clunk cough cough kerplunk. Nope it ain't working me old mate. Right at that moment a sailor appears off the port bow of my distressed car and says: 'You need to get moving, matey. There are people behind you here trying to get off the ship.'

'Oh really!' (You see I'm not blind). 'The car won't start – I don't know if you've noticed. And not being a mechanic, I haven't a clue what's wrong with it.'

'Here Phil,' calls the sailor to his mate, 'give us an 'and to push this 'eap off the boat.'

They begin the arduous and embarrassing task of pushing

my car, my wife, and my baby daughter off their precious boat.

'Where can I find a mechanic or a garage?' I ask the sailor with a little disdain in my now extremely irritated voice.

'As it 'appens guv, there is a geezer down the road, there by the dock, who's open all night. Per'aps he can give you an 'and. I'd say this though, if you was asking me, which you ain't, you've got a problem with your oil.'

'How do you know that then?' I hiss.

'It's all over the floor, matey.'

We manage to push my tin wreck down the road, to the garage mentioned by my friend the sailor. It's almost Dickensian in appearance and looks like it hasn't been modernised at all in the last century. It could have been owned by Ebenezer Scrooge, it had that sort of feel about it. I felt like asking the guy if I could fetch some coal to put on the non-existent fire. It's old, dank, dark and kind of spooky, but hey this is now 2 a.m. and beggars can't be choosers.

'Qu'est-ce que c'est le problem m'sieur?'

Jo begins a rapid diatribe in fluent French as to our requirements on this cold and very dark winter's night.

Before you can say 'spanner in the works', the mechanic has the entire car on a hoist, and is looking deep into the recesses of the engine and its working parts. It takes all of 3 minutes for him to give us his diagnosis.

'You 'ave no oil pemmp m'sieur!' declares Jules Verne.

'Pemmp?' I say confused.

'I think you'll find he means "pump" David – oil pump.'

Oh right. Groovy, fantastic, brilliant, fandabidozi.

'He has just told me it'll take about 5 days to get zee pump from England and fiiiiix it,' declares Jo, now also getting just a tad miffed.

'What are we going to do then?'

'What are we supposed to do in moments like thiiiis, David?' says Jo. 'We pray! That's what we do. Father in heaven, You know the situation we are in right now. We have at least 1,000 kilometres to drive. We have no oil, no pump and the situation iiiis in the natural impossible. We are asking You now Jesus for a miracle. Please Lord, if it be Your will, let us continue our journey, in the name of Jesus we ask. Amen.'

I look at Jo and she looks at me for the briefest of seconds.

'Come on then, let's go,' she says.

Such faith!

And just like that, the car is lowered, oil is placed in the system, the key is turned and the car starts first time.

We drive 1,000 kilometres all the way to Jo's parents place, with no oil pump. We arrive very very tired on 21 December, ready to start the Christmas festivities with Jo's family, who are all gathered for the holidays.

When we rise the following morning, everyone is there. Pierre and Jean-Michel (known as 'Mickey' to everyone) who are Jo's two brothers, her sister Sabine, Guy and Lucienne, Jo's parents, and the three of us, all there around the breakfast table, chatting excitedly about the season, making all sorts of arrangements for the coming days. Christmas is such a joyous time to spend with family, to be able to share, confide, laugh, smile; it has to rank as my favourite time of year.

'Où sont tes pantoufles David?' (where are your slippers David?) demands Lucienne. Jo's mum is speaking her language in a slow drawl, so I can understand what she is saying.

'I don't have any,' I reply, looking at Jo to make sure I have given the correct response. (I didn't speak French at all well and Jo's parents couldn't speak a word of English.)

'We must buy him some when we go to town today Pierre,' Lucienne says to my brother-in-law who is busily dunking some 'biscotte' in his cocoa. Little Natasha, my baby daughter, is sitting on Lucienne's lap playing with the buttons on her cardigan.

By 9:30 a.m. that same morning, Lucienne, Jo's mum, is dead and her brother Pierre is seriously injured in one of the most horrific car accidents the town of Annemasse has ever seen.

As I lay in my bed in my hotel room reflecting on this and other awesome events in my history, I realised that God's love had been poured into my life at a very young age. I was 6 years old, when, at an evangelistic crusade led by Eric Hutchings at the Colston Hall in Bristol, I had stood up and received Jesus Christ into my heart as my Lord and Saviour. However, by the time I had reached 16 years old, I felt I knew better than God regarding how to conduct my life. It was at this period of my life that I wandered from the pathway He had set out for me. Where was His love during this period? Well, quite simply, He was waiting for me, standing there all the time, waiting for me to realise, to understand, to feel His love and presence in my life. My Lord had a long long wait. It wasn't until I reached the age of 38 did I finally and completely dedicate my life to Him and His service, and in all that time my Saviour didn't go anywhere. He just simply waited for me, loving me all the time. It seems so strange now, looking back – His love was shining so brightly, why hadn't I seen it?

As a young man I was involved in the entertainment industry as a disc jockey, working in nightclubs all over the place. I was good at what I did and very successful, too. Drugs were available to most of my colleagues, as were women, in vast quantities.

I remember on many many occasions going to different friends' houses to buy drugs – speed, dope, all sorts – only to find out that they had 'just run out'. I never ever could get hooked on these drugs no matter how I tried. It was as if I was on a downward spiral of destruction and rebellion. However, the Lord had other plans. He had His hand firmly and truly on my life. My parents prayed every day for me for 25 years. Every single day without fail, they would include me in their prayers. God clearly had His hand on my life all this time. It was as if I was a mouse with a long tail and God had placed His finger on it. I could run around in circles and that was all. No more than that. The Lord had put His hand in the way when I tried to grapple the mountain leading to my destruction. He simply would not let me go. I know many people would say that this doesn't hold up in the Bible but I can only describe to you what happened in my life and how God has always been there for me.

CHAPTER 5

FOR I KNOW THE PLANS
I HAVE FOR YOU

The next day at the Marriott when I went down for breakfast, Simon, who had almost finished eating, greeted me. He welcomed me warmly as he always did.

'David, did you sleep well?' he asked in his rather endearing Scandinavian accent.

'I did, Simon, thank you,' I replied with genuine affection.

'I'm going for a long walk along the beach after breakfast with Edward John, would you like to join us?'

I'd hate that, I thought.

'I'd love to,' said I with copious amounts of enthusiasm. You see the truth is, gentle reader, I have never been one for taking lots of exercise. I do it if I have to, but out of choice, I'd rather watch paint dry.

'What time are we going?'

'As soon as you have finished eating your eggs and bacon,' said Simon with a hint of disapproval as he had just consumed rabbit food, yogurt and green tea. *Green tea? What on earth is that? That can't be for usual consumption. Aha! must be for Scandinavians then.*

We chatted about this and that. We discussed the previous evening's broadcast and got onto the subject of the prophetic word given to me by Edward John in the car. Simon asked me how it was impacting me. I told him in no uncertain terms that I felt it had completely changed my life. I was looking forward to spending more time with him and Edward. You see, I didn't know Edward as well as I wanted to, and I realised he didn't know me that well either. We had on numerous occasions shared morsels from each other's lives, but no real relationship had developed. However, I knew Edward was a 'real man of God': someone who followed the Lord very closely, not making a move without His almighty blessing.

Edward John had told me previously, that at 17 years old when he had dedicated his life to God, he had asked the Lord for three things:

1. That he always had plenty of coffee
2. That he always had clothes to wear
3. That he always had the necessary airline tickets to do the job.

God has always provided these things for Edward in miraculous ways, each time he has needed them. Just listening to the stories of how the Lord has touched his life is so inspiring in itself. It is incredible. That is Edward's story, however, and I have no doubt in my mind that he will one day share it.

After breakfast we all met up in the reception area of the hotel. I must confess I had a little look to see if the lads were prepared for a long walk. I was expecting to see hiking boots and back packs along with those windcheaters. We were only going for a stroll on the beach. A stroll! We walked for Britain that day. We must have walked at least 5 miles. Phew! I get tired just remembering.

As we walked and talked we discussed the previous evening. We talked and talked all three of us about everything under the sun. It was at this time that Edward began telling me about a friend of his who had memorised the entire book of Mark (one of the Gospels in the Bible) and that he had presented it on stage as a piece of drama. As he talked I was already seeing the production in my mind's eye. It began to unfold in its raw state to begin with. As the day unravelled, so did this drama presentation with all the details coming into view. I was so excited. I could hardly contain myself.

The walk to the pier was quite tough with the boys swinging their hips as though this were an Olympic event! It was hard keeping up. I puffed and blowed. Lagging behind them now and again, I would stop to shout things like, 'Oh look at that! Isn't it wonderful?' – purely a ruse to catch my wheezing breath. I laugh now when I think about it because the walk back was entirely different. I walked alongside the boys with a new spring in my step, really enjoying the exercise and the company.

Edward was explaining that he would be leaving the hotel at about 2 p.m. to fly back to Norway and as it was now 12 p.m. we had little time to talk, discuss and plan. I remember saying to Edward that I was going to write a show on 'love' featuring all the relevant scriptures I could find from the Bible. It would contain music and other dramatic effects. In fact, I couldn't wait to get started on this wonderful, worthwhile project. It was as if I was on fire and I needed to burn and burn.

When we got back to the hotel we ordered coffee while Simon went upstairs for a rest. (There you go then – I'm not the only one who needs to take a rest every so often.) Eddie and I (I call him Eddie now as we are friends) sat in the reception area to discuss more details of the show.

'I'm going to call this show *"O Love That Will Not Let Me Go"*,' I cried. I felt as if I was having an epiphany. 'I'll start with the famous hymn written by George Matheson. The words just say everything I'm feeling at the moment.'

O joy that seekest me through pain,
I cannot close my heart to thee;
I trace the rainbow through the rain,
And feel the promise is not vain,
That morn shall tearless be.

You know something? As soon as you come up with the beginning, the rest starts to fall into place. I could really begin to see in my mind's eye the whole production. I'll tell you something else, too, I was speaking to my TV producer Don Heginbotham on another matter, and I felt like running the idea past him to get his view. He totally concurred with me that it was firstly from God and secondly that it would be awesome.

Oh how I love You Jesus for the blessings You bestow on Your children every day. The mercies You show are new every morning.

Chapter 6

Plans To Prosper You And Not To Harm You

'Where are these tears coming from Lord?' I whispered to God as I drove along the road a few days later. I had been crying and weeping for an eternity it seemed to me. In actual fact, it was more like 3 days. I was heading back down the A1 on my way home to dear old Essex. I was feeling incredibly peaceful and serene. There was no anger in me at all. Listen! Here I am in the outside lane on the A1, and yes, another lorry driver has decided to pull out in front of me to pass yet another truck. And yes, he is taking an eternity to pass this lumbering vehicle. I'm stuck behind him, in floods of tears, and really not caring if I am there all day. Let me explain what a miracle this is. Only a few days ago, at this point I would usually be very close to losing my composure. (I say this politely. What I really mean is that I would be seriously thinking of some way to end the lorry driver's life – they were my pet hate.) Oh come on now, I'm not the only one and I know you must have one or two.

It is purely from God when you experience the sort of favour I was going through. The tears would come and go. I would be listening to something on the radio and suddenly, for no apparent reason at all, I would begin to speak in tongues as the Holy Spirit gave me utterance. There's nothing quite like it: basking in the presence of Almighty God.

My mind began to wander once again as I remembered something from my past: something that happened to me a few years ago as I drove to the local town where I lived.

It is now 1995, early morning and I'm driving toward Basildon when the presence of the Lord fills my car. I feel an amazing sense of Jesus sitting by my side as I drive. His love is all over me. I burst into tears as I feel my Jesus comforting me, saying nothing, just loving me. I am still driving, almost at my destination. I decide to go and have a coffee in a café near by. As I arrive at this eatery, there's a large, heavy, overweight guy with a huge protruding belly, obviously the proprietor, standing confidently behind a decrepit, moth-eaten counter. Actually, he is swearing rather profusely at some innocent little boy. Hearing his words is grieving my spirit. It is offending me in a way I have never noticed before. A lone mother with her youngster in tow is drinking a cup of coffee. She is constantly sniping at her child, who I believe is very well behaved. The boy's mother is really annoyed with him now and screams at him to go outside, 'Out of my sight!' she hollers. There I see him as he kicks a stone lying on the pavement. The tears course down his face. He looks dejected, forlorn.

I remember, before I had gone into town that morning, I had been having a quiet time with God and read somewhere in a book, 'Ask the Lord how much He loves the world.' This I believe was His response, because the tears began to fall again in earnest. So much so, I had to leave the café and get to my car as soon as physically possible. I drove home and on arrival I remember my wife asking me, 'What on earth is the matter with you?'

I recount the story of all that had happened to me.

'I need to write this down, love,' I sob, the tears cascading down my face. 'My heart is broken, really broken.' I feel moved to commit the memory to verse.

The words I uttered to my God
That day, they were so real
'Show me Lord,' my heart expounded
'The full extent of the love You feel.'

I found this café, dismal, dank
I sat back in the chair.
The large dejected man in charge
Brings tea to me and swears.

I sat alone; I'd found the time
To ponder on this life,
To my chagrin, he shouts loud
His words are like a knife.

They're aimed at the little ones
They can't have done him wrong.
This man, he hates with sharpened words
That's why I write this song.

The mother shouts oaths of curse
The little boy, he screams.
She tells him what she thinks of him
And throws him out, it seems.

The child, he looks forlorn and lost
His face is streaked with tears.
'What have I done and at what cost?'
His cry is fraught with fears.

I got up from my table when
My heart it swelled with love.
My eyes they filled with tears of pain
It felt so hard to move.

'My God, my God, what happened there?'
I cried to Him above,
'Why has that child felt so much grief?
He's little, he craves love.'

'Now My son you understand,
You comprehend My pain,
You love that child; I love the world,
That treats Me just the same.
You love that child; I love the world,
The world I'll gain again.'

Isn't the Lord wonderful? Isn't it great the way Jesus shows us the road signs as soon as we diligently ask Him? So why didn't I remember this afterwards? Why did I forget the lesson my Father in Heaven taught me? Well, I believe circumstances of life begin to creep in. These problems and the trials of life stop us from enjoying the fullness of what Christ has for us, for what God has in store for us; all of us. God loves us so much that He sent His Son to save the world from the destruction that would have come, had He not acted. He must have been in such pain Himself when He saw His son dying on the cross. For a second, God the Father turned His face away. Seeing His Son on the tree must have been so hard. But it was for us He did that. He sacrificed His only Son for you and me, so that we would be reconciled to

God, allowing us to go to Him for forgiveness. What love. Such love.

One day, not so very long after that incident at the café, I was driving home. As I approached my house, I began crying once again, this time it wasn't gentle weeping, but hard and fast tears. I didn't have any understanding as to why I should be in this state. Not 5 minutes before I'd been fine, in fact I had been in fine fettle, but suddenly, and with no explanation, I began to sob my heart out. It was almost impossible to steer the little car, as I weaved along the small lane leading to my house.

'Why am I crying, Lord?' I screamed at the top of my voice.

'You are a casualty of war, My son,' declared my Saviour in words of great love and compassion.

My dear friend, you need to be fully protected by the blood of the Lamb of God at all times. We must make it a practice to put on the full armour of God every day to protect us from the fiery darts Satan will throw at us at any given opportunity, especially if we are not walking close to our Lord and Saviour.

Finally, be strong in the Lord and in his mighty power. Put on the full armour of God so that you can take your stand against the devil's schemes. For our struggle is not

against flesh and blood, but against the rulers, against the authorities, against the powers of this dark world and against the spiritual forces of evil in the heavenly realms. Therefore put on the full armour of God, so that when the day of evil comes, you may be able to stand your ground, and after you have done everything, to stand. Stand firm then, with the belt of truth buckled round your waist, with the breastplate of righteousness in place, and with your feet fitted with the readiness that comes from the gospel of peace. In addition to all this, take up the shield of faith, with which you can extinguish all the flaming arrows of the evil one. Take the helmet of salvation and the sword of the Spirit, which is the word of God. And pray in the Spirit on all occasions with all kinds of prayers and requests. With this in mind, be alert and always keep on praying for all the saints.
(Ephesians 6:10–18)

May I briefly, very briefly, share some thoughts with you on unconditional love? This is so important at this point in the book and indeed in your journey. If not, then skip the next page or so and get right into the stories again. The Greek word for this type of love is 'agape'. I'm so pleased there is another word to describe this feeling, this sentiment, for it perfectly describes the Father's love for us, for you and me. Saying the words 'I love you' gives one all sorts of different thoughts. For instance, lovers speak these three words in intimate moments. Mothers who watch a child excel at a sport, or pass an examination speak them. Grandmas, who see their offspring swimming for the first time, say them with joy. A father, who watches on the sideline as his son scores his first goal with the school team and mouths 'I'm so proud of you'. These are words of love. But it does beg a question. Each time these words are used, what price must be paid for them to be spoken? What do I have to do to achieve your love, to earn it even? Is there a hidden agenda to these words? This is not agape love, it is not unconditional. Well, God loves us totally free of any condition. There are no hidden agendas with God, none whatsoever. The price for this love has been paid, gentle reader, by Jesus on the cross at Calvary. I'm sure you have seen the movie *The Passion of The Christ*, Mel Gibson's brilliant and highly acclaimed portrayal of the last week of our Lord's life on earth. Well, if you watch it again, wait until you see the suffering our Lord endured for you and me, as depicted in this powerful film, then bear in mind that He went through so much more than is shown on screen. The Bible tells us that He was unrecognisable, that He was rejected, beaten, scourged and nailed to a cross for your sins and for mine. For you and me! I can't imagine the power of the love that would drive someone to do that for me, so that I can stand before God on the day of judgement, sinless and guiltless when really, in reality, I deserve death and hell. It is too awesome to believe. I just wanted to say this, so that it would sink into your spirit and reside there for ever.

Ephesians 3:16–19 says this:

I pray that out of his glorious riches he may strengthen you with power through his Spirit in your inner being, so that Christ may dwell in your hearts through faith. And I pray that you, being rooted and established in love, may have power, together with all the saints, to grasp how wide and long and high and deep is the love of Christ, and to know that this love that surpasses knowledge – that you may be filled to the measure of all the fulness of God.

Does that begin to explain God's awesome love for you and how He feels for you?

CHAPTER 7

PLANS TO GIVE YOU A HOPE AND A FUTURE

The tears of passion, compassion and love continued all that week, hardly stopping for even the slightest of breaks. I was being filled constantly with God's love and compassion. I was preparing to go to work that Saturday morning. As I mentioned before, I work for a radio station in London and present a programme based on reading passages of scripture for people who request them for whatever reason. The programme is always 'anointed' as the Lord's word will never return to Him void (Isaiah 55:11). I must say that I certainly didn't think it was my presentation skills that cut the mustard.

Whenever I go to work in London, I always ride my motorbike as it's much easier to park and to manoeuvre round the traffic, so imagine my surprise when travelling on the famous A13 toward the studio, I began yet again to cry. The tears were streaming down my face the entire journey. Have you ever cried with a helmet on and the visor down? It was during this journey I felt the Lord say to me very clearly, 'Tell My people about this love you have experienced.'

Whoa! I thought to myself, *that's awesome, that ties into what I felt at the beginning of the week regarding writing the show.*

I duly arrived at the studio in a peaceful mood, not the usual boisterous step this morning. I knew, that I knew, that I knew, that I had been healed inside of all the hurt and pain I had carried around for years. It had at last found its way to the garbage. It was like realising the dustman had collected the rubbish. Something that had been mounting up for weeks and weeks had been dumped into a celestial garbage truck and removed once and for all. What a great feeling, knowing that your problems are now in the hands of Almighty God.

As I sat at my computer to begin the pre-production work I needed to do before my programme, I began to think about my mum.

'Mum?' I asked one morning, while I was staying with her and my father, 'Do you love me?'

I was 25 years old and about to get divorced from the woman I thought I would always love. I was in a rather heartbroken state, a bit of a mess you might say. So asking the question seemed a little strange to say the least. My marriage breakdown was mostly my fault. Maybe I was just too young and immature and needed my mum. I stood in the front room of the family home in Cornwall, and my mother was in the kitchen.

'I'm not sure what love is, David.'

Eh! Did I hear right? I think to myself. *So she doesn't love me after all. Is this why I am in so much pain at the moment?*

Thinking of that little scene brought more tears as I tried to concentrate on work, but it began to answer some questions in my life. (Thinking of my mum always did that for me.) We still speak on the phone at least twice a month. I had felt for quite a while that she and I had no connection at all. That maybe I was adopted. Once I even asked her if I was. She told me that I was being silly as I looked like my cousin far too much to not belong to the family.

The Lord has brought to my mind since then, little scenes with my mum when I was tiny, about 3 or 4 years old, where I would ask her to play a tune that I loved on the piano. I can see her doing that now, smiling down at me as her slim and elegant fingers glide over the keys of the piano that stood in the lounge.

I love my hair being stroked with long finger nails, much to the annoyance of my children. All four of them have had to sit and stroke my hair at some time or another over the years. As a child, my mother would do this to me when I was in the throws of yet another asthma attack.

So she does love me Lord.

'Yes, in her way she does.'

Oh blessed Jesus, thank You for that.

I rang her up the other day on the Lord's instruction to ask her the same question I had asked all those years ago. She answered me with almost exactly the same words. She doesn't remember me asking her when I was 25, but that's OK. I said what I believed the Lord had told me to say: 'Mum, it doesn't matter if you don't love *me,* darling, I'll love *you* for both of us.'

As I sat at my computer preparing for *Worship Hour,* I realised something else, too. I knew that I was exactly in the place the Lord wanted me to be, doing His will, His work, for His service. I felt deep in the recesses of my heart that today's programme was going to be an exceptional blessing to those who tuned in to listen.

From the moment the programme started, until it was over, God was completely in control. The music, all of it, was engineered by Him (it is all computerised), the readings I brought all manufactured by the Lord. I was in 'freefall'. I could do no wrong. It was fantastic. Needless to say, gentle reader, I wept all the way through the programme, too. On occasion I found it really difficult to talk as I battled through the tears, but there were listeners who were being mightily released from past pain and hurt.

It is so wonderful to be used by the Lord in such a powerful way.

A few weeks after, I felt led to make a call for salvation on the radio. Three people responded and committed their lives to Christ. That truly is a miracle.

Chapter 8

Then You Will Call On Me And Come And Pray To Me

As I write this book, I have been asking the Lord to give me favour in sharing things with you that mean so much to me on my journey of self-discovery. Memories that I thought had long ago disappeared from the annals of my mind start to flood back. I think that this particular week in my life I have been sharing with you, was without doubt the most impacting 7 days I have ever experienced. And I can only give the honour and the glory for the work He has done to our Lord and Saviour Jesus Christ, without whom all this would mean naught.

I remember very vividly disappearing to a wonderful place in North Lincolnshire called Epworth, the very place where in 1703 the founder of Methodism, John Wesley, was born. This place is very spiritual and the region is simply beautiful and very peaceful.

It was in this setting that I sat down to write the show of *O Love That Will Not Let Me Go*. I need to tell you at this point, that as I started to write, I realised I had to pray and 'release to the Lord' someone who was very special to me. What do I mean by that? When we hold something against another person, or even when God brings someone to mind that is somehow connected to us in an un-godly way, the Lord will sometimes gently ask us to release that person into His almighty care so that the burden is lifted from our shoulders. Occasionally, people or situations come into our lives that we inadvertently put above or before our relationship with God, with the result that our eyes are taken from the Master. Once when I had done that I felt really ill. I had palpitations, I was clammy and just felt awful. I didn't have a clue what was going on, as to why I felt so bad. I felt like retreating back to my house as quickly as possible. I wanted to return to the familiar, to that which I was used to, my surroundings, the things and people I knew. It was overwhelming. However, I continued to write and seek God's word all through this. He came through for me in a wonderful way, by reminding me of Jeremiah 29:11–14 which says,

'For I know the plans I have for you,' declares the Lord, 'plans to prosper you and not to harm you, plans to give you hope and a future. Then you will call upon me and come and pray to me, and I will listen to you. You will seek me and find me when you seek me with all your heart. I will be found by you,' declares the Lord, 'and will bring you back from captivity.'

What an encouragement! The Lord was in the middle of doing a new thing with me – I had never ever written a show by myself before. In the past, I have always worked on this sort of thing in collaboration with other people. This then, indeed was a new thing. I could feel that the anointing was certainly on this project. I remember, too, that when I made the journey to Oslo to see Edward John, and as soon as I began working on this project again in his apartment, I began to feel ill, the same sort of feeling, except this time I had pains across my chest as well. I remember asking Edward, 'Can we go out and get a breath of fresh air? Or have a drive in the car?'

We went out straight away and as we drove through the beautiful and historic streets of Oslo I started to feel much worse. I shared this with Edward. He then told me what had happened to him while on the way to pick me up from the airport. Firstly, he told me that when he went to buy some petrol at a gas station, and after he had paid the bill, the car wouldn't start. He struggled with the VW Golf for 15 minutes until it finally fired up. Apparently, some moisture had gotten into the system. He told me in no uncertain terms that this had never ever happened before. Interesting eh?! What really got to me though was when he told me that he thought he was having a heart attack on the way to the airport. Let me firstly deal with this one. Eddie is 35 years old and at the peak of physical fitness. He trains every day so for him to feel that was remarkable. To match that, he arrived at the airport very late. This is not usual for him. He is always on time. However, he got completely lost on his way to collect me. This, too, was impossible. In fact, when he first recounted this tale to his wonderful mother (whom I immediately loved when I met her for the first time the evening I arrived in Oslo), she declared that it wasn't possible either. Eddie knows the area so well. What do you think, gentle reader? Is this coincidence? I don't believe so. I believe it was a spiritual attack. The evil one, who is our enemy, doesn't want the show to be produced or even to be discussed. 1 John 4:18 says this, 'There is no fear in love. But perfect love drives out fear, because fear has to do with punishment. The one who fears is not made perfect in love.' This is why I believe that the show of *O Love That Will Not Let Me Go* is awesome and life-changing for anyone who accepts the truth: that Jesus loves them so completely and utterly that their life must and will change.

Whilst on the subject of love, the following has just popped into my mind. I think it is a wonderful test and I believe that the Lord has put it on my heart to convey to you. Think of a loved one, someone you are very close to. It could be your wife/husband, your best friend, your mother/father or both, someone who means the world to you. In fact, test this against all of them. 1 Corinthians 13:4–8 is, I believe, the perfect blueprint for what love really is. It's not just an emotion but so much more. Here are those verses for you:

> Love is patient, love is kind. It does not envy, it does not boast, it is not proud. It is not rude, it is not self-seeking, it is not easily angered, it keeps no record of wrongs. Love does not delight in evil but rejoices with the truth. It always protects, always trusts, always hopes, always perseveres. Love never fails.

It is a fantastic test. I've tried it myself. With some people in my life I am certainly left wanting. With others, however, I can achieve this. I know that in my life I need to achieve this with everyone I come into contact with.

Someone very close to me recounted a story of a party she was going to with her two children, who incidentally were both adults at the time. She told me that as she was making her way toward this party on New Year's Eve, she spotted a tramp sitting in the street. He was rubbing his feet. As she walked past, she felt a compelling urge to walk back to him. She asked him what he would do if she gave him some money. He replied immediately, 'I would buy some jelly.'

Patricia said to him, very quietly, 'Remember this: when the clock strikes twelve midnight, there will be a woman in Sheffield who will be loving you very much.' And with that, she gave him some money and upped and left.

Is that not a picture of what real love is? Of how we should view others on this planet of ours? Is this not what the Lord meant when He said, 'Love each other as I have loved you. Greater love has no-one than this, that he lay down his life for his friends' (John 15:12,13).

How many of us would have done that? How many of us would do that for Jesus?

Here is some further food for thought: I was once at a conference in Sunderland and a guy called Marc Dupont was speaking, who was a prophet. During the service, he said to the congregation that 20 per cent of the people in the audience would suffer death for the sake of their faith in the Lord Jesus Christ. I wondered as I sat and listened that day, how many people were saying to themselves, 'Let it not be me Lord, I'm not willing to do that at all.' And on the other hand how many responded by saying, 'Here I am Lord, send me.' I now ask you, my friend, the same question. How would you respond?

CHAPTER 9

I WILL LISTEN TO YOU

Every morning since all of what I have written happened, I try to get a quiet time with the Lord and He reveals things to me all the time. He keeps pouring His love out on me; letting me know that all is well, that He has His hand on all things, in other words, God is in total control of my life. 'Why?!' I hear you ask. I'm glad you asked that question. It's because I have given Him permission to be in control. I have declared to my Lord that I cannot do life, live, exist even, without Him.

I remember years ago now when I was about 24 or 25, when I was living at home with my parents after my first marriage breakdown, my mum asked me if I would like to accompany her to a 'revival, renewal' meeting in Truro. I said I would go with her. I have no idea why I said I would as it really didn't interest me at all. I thought that I would be listening to all the stuff I had heard before on many occasions. *This is going to be interesting*, I mused to myself when we were setting off.

When we duly arrived at the venue in Truro, we were greeted by the usual Christianeeze language that seemed to pour from these 'saints', 'do gooders', 'holier than thou' people, (at least, gentle reader, that is how I perceived them back then). You know the type of thing I'm talking about here don't you?

'Welcome brother.'

Brother? I'm not your brother.

'God bless you richly.'

Well, he ain't blessed me so far mate!

'May you hear that still, small voice this evening.'

Looking back, my responses then surprise me now, when I think of God's almighty grace in my life. He had blessed me not 2 years earlier when my ex-wife and I had witnessed the miracle of the oil pump and the 'no oil' situation. Do you remember? Well why would my response be so glib?

My mum and I sat down waiting for the 'worship team' to do their thing. We were going to be listening to hymns done in the 'modern way'. As they started, I was thinking to myself, *What on earth are you doing here? Get out now, this is dangerous.* Why should I think that? I'd been going to church all my life, for as long as I can remember. I had been in church sometimes three times on a Sunday as I was growing up. So why this reaction now? What was going on? The feelings grew and grew as I tried very hard to join in with the singing. It was getting unbearable. It was horrible. 'Get out now, David!' I heard on my inside.

I can try to describe this feeling thus. Imagine you are sitting in your classroom at school, and the teacher runs a fingernail down the blackboard. Remember that feeling inside as your body shivers? Imagine if you will, the drip drip drip of a tap that is not completely turned off at night, and you are trying to sleep. Imagine if someone beside you is snoring so loudly that all you want to do is scream. Do you get the picture now? Well that was how I was feeling listening to these people singing. I had to get out. I did – I ran as fast as I could outside to have a cigarette. It was awful.

Why was it awful? Well simply because Satan was on my inside screaming for me to get out, because it didn't line up with what he wanted for my life. However, the Holy Spirit wanted me to stay and I was feeling no peace at all from Him. I think this was the period in my life when I realised for the first time that there was such a thing as a spiritual battle raging on the inside of us. Maybe you are feeling this as you read this book. Do you want to run away from God, or do you want the Lord to get the victory over the things in your life that need to be and – be honest – *have* to be sorted out?

I now realise on reflection that God was crying out to me, to let Him take control of my troubled life. I wish, oh how I wish, I had heeded that cry all those years ago. Because even then, the Lord loved me, as a troubled father looks on his son when he has turned away from what he should be doing and where he should be. The story (or parable as the Bible would call it) of 'The Lost Son' comes immediately to mind. A powerful illustration of how God the Father looks on us at times in our lives when we have wandered off the pathway that He has mapped out for us.

Then he said, 'There was once a man who had two sons. The younger said to his father, "Father, I want right now what's coming to me."

'So the father divided the property between them. It wasn't long before the younger son packed his bags and left for a distant country. There, undisciplined and dissipated, he wasted everything he had. After he had gone through all his money, there was a bad famine all through that country and he began to hurt. He signed on with a citizen there who assigned him to his fields to slop the pigs. He was so hungry he would have eaten the corncobs in the pig slop, but no one would give him any.

'That brought him to his senses. He said, "All those farmhands working for my father sit down to three meals a day, and here I am starving to death. I'm going back to my father. I'll say to him, Father, I've sinned against God, I've sinned before you; I don't deserve to be called your son. Take me on as a hired hand." He got right up and went home to his father.

'When he was still a long way off, his father saw him. His heart pounding, he ran out, embraced him, and kissed him. The son started his speech: "Father, I've sinned against God, I've sinned before you; I don't deserve to be called your son ever again."

'But the father wasn't listening. He was calling to the servants, "Quick. Bring a clean set of clothes and dress him. Put the family ring on his finger and sandals on his feet. Then get a grain-fed heifer and roast it. We're going to feast! We're going to have a wonderful time! My son is here – given up for dead and now alive! Given up for lost and now found!" And they began to have a wonderful time.

'All this time his older son was out in the field. When the day's work was done he came in. As he approached the house, he heard the music and dancing. Calling over one of the houseboys, he asked what was going on. He told him, "Your brother came home. Your father has ordered a feast – barbecued beef! – because he has him home safe and sound."

'The older brother stalked off in an angry sulk and refused to join in. His father came out and tried to talk to him, but he wouldn't listen. The son said, "Look how many years I've stayed here serving you, never giving you one moment of grief, but have you ever thrown a party for me and my friends? Then this son of yours who has thrown away your money on whores shows up and you go all out with a feast!"

'His father said, "Son, you don't understand. You're with me all the time, and everything that is mine is yours

– but this is a wonderful time, and we had to celebrate. This brother of yours was dead, and he's alive! He was lost, and he's found!'"

(Luke 15:11–32, *The Message*)

Isn't God great in how He treats us, when we've clearly been going so badly wrong? This is because of the unconditional love He has for us: the all-consuming 'agape'.

Do you mind that I share so candidly with you what has been going on in my life? The reason I feel this is important, is that this has been my journey thus far, and I feel that by sharing with you so frankly, you might recognise some pitfalls and steer the direction of your life the way the Father wants you to go. Oh how I wish I had heeded all the warnings my Father in heaven gave me across the years. Where would I be now? How would my life have changed?

What I feel is more important now, however, is that you, my dear friend, listen to the still, small voice of our Lord, and share with others the love you feel that comes from the very throne room of glory.

CHAPTER 10

YOU WILL SEEK ME AND FIND ME WHEN YOU SEEK ME WITH ALL YOUR HEART

In this chapter, I want to dwell on the 'father heart of God' for a moment or two. The reason? Because, I believe that once you are in perfect tune with the Lord's heart, and begin to understand how a true father should treat his children, then the obviousness of God's love can become paramount.

One way I can begin to show you how this has affected me, is to try to convey to you the sort of relationship I had with my own father. He was a wonderful man but has been dead now for some years. I still miss him a lot and think of him whenever I play my piano. There is a photograph of him in a frame that sits on top of the instrument and it's almost as if he looks at me approvingly as I play. We always had a healthy rivalry in the area of music. You see, I was born with the wonderful gift of perfect pitch. What that means is, simply, that I can hear harmonies as people sing. I can pitch notes correctly whatever key they are in, and moreover, I can play the piano by ear without having to constantly refer to the music. Now my dad didn't have that gift so he would constantly challenge me, especially when it came to chords we would each play. There was a constant banter going on between us.

'That is the wrong chord you played there, David,' he would say to me with a huge smile on his rugged features.

'Show me then, Dad,' would be my immediate response, clearly with a hint of sarcasm.

He would ring me up at the most inopportune moments and tell me a joke. He would say the punchline and before I would get a chance to laugh, he would hang up on me.

One time, I remember, when I was about 6 years old or so, my mum and dad, my three brothers and my sister were going to the countryside near our home for a fun day and a picnic. It was a Sunday and my father was due to be preaching at a little country church nearby to where we were having our picnic. (He was a lay preacher on a circuit in Bristol and preached most Sunday evenings.)

As Dad drove off in the car, going to preach, Mum decided she was going to join in the game of cricket we had begun. My sister was only a babe in arms, so she was in her pram. We were having a great time, enjoying each other's company. There's the usual boisterous behaviour from the boys. As I'm the youngest boy it usually fell on me to get the blame. I was always the scapegoat if there was any trouble going. It was, however, always in good fun.

'When can I bat?' I complained, as it seemed to me that I hardly ever got a turn. Batting was always my most favourite thing.

'When you run after the ball faster, David,' shouted my brother Chris at the top of his voice. 'You really are useless at this game, totally useless.' *Oh how I wish I was good at cricket.* I am a bit of a duffer at the game I must admit. *If only I could impress him.* I was always in awe of my brother Chris. He was so cool, and so naughty. *Oh how I wish I could rebel like him.* Just at that moment, my dad returned from his preaching engagement.

'How have you managed to get back so quickly, Alan?' my mother Joyce asked him.

'When I arrived at the church, Joyce, there was someone else conducting the service. I couldn't believe that I had made a mistake, so I left. Not much point in staying, not when my boys are out here playing cricket. Come on Simon,' shouts my father, 'throw me the ball, I'll bowl.'

All too soon and it's time to pack up the bails and wickets and wend our weary way home.

'Come on boys, you've all got school in the morning, you'll be tired if we don't go home now.'

We were driving home and had reached the suburb of Patchway when my mother cried, 'Look!' with mirth in her voice. We all turned to our left to see a little church. There we all read the sign:

PATCHWAY METHODIST CHURCH

Preaching this evening:

ALAN R. ALDOUS

Needless to say, the church was shut, all dark. My father had gone to the wrong church to preach that night.

I must have been about 4 years old, when one evening on returning from a vacation in Cornwall at Prah Sands, where we used to go every year, my father stopped the car, a vintage Armstrong Sidley, at a fish and chip shop. He was going in to buy us all some wonderful fish and chips and 'scrumps'. Yummmm. As he stood in line waiting his turn to be served, I asked my mum a very pointed question. 'Mummy,' I whispered, so my brothers couldn't hear me, 'What does N O P A R K I N G mean?'

My dad was always fair but sometimes tough. He would punish us when we did wrong. He would also love us when we needed to be loved and cared for. If we 'messed around' with Mum and she said the words, 'Wait until your father comes home,' it would drive real fear into me. My body would tremble as I realised that the punishment would be most likely painful and decisive. As I reflect now, I realise that usually that punishment was warranted. I deserved it, as did my siblings.

What did I love about my dad? Many things really. Quite often if he had punished me, depending on the 'offence', he would come to my room and ask, 'Have you learned your lesson, David?' I would immediately cry and promise that I had. He was such a wonderful man.

At my daddy's funeral when he died a few years ago now, I remember my uncle speaking about my dad, and what he had done in life. The congregation were in fits of laughter as he recounted story after story of my dad, and what he had got up to during his lifetime.

My father preached the word of God for 30 years until he and Mum had an encounter with the awesome power of the Holy Spirit in 1968, which completely and radically changed their lives.

I look back on my dad's life and smile as I recall him. I would love to think that my relationship with God is so much more than my relationship with my earthly father, but what a blueprint to look at. If I have been even a quarter as good as my dad in my parenting skills toward my four children then I have been successful. My kids can then begin their journey into understanding the father heart of God.

If your relationship with your father isn't good, perhaps you didn't have a father to speak of, then please, just for a moment, imagine how a perfect father should behave toward his children. When you do this, you begin to see into the father heart of God. You begin to feel the Lord's very heartbeat, as it beats in tune with yours; just for you. Isn't this then His love manifest in our lives?

CHAPTER 11

TWO ARE UNITED INTO ONE

Jane, my wife, has always been fiercely independent, much to my annoyance. But she had to be, had no choice: she was foisted off to boarding school at age 11 through no fault of hers. While there, she had to learn very quickly that life sometimes was not fair.

When I met Jane I was at my lowest ebb. I was living and working in the South of France, as was she. My first marriage had collapsed due to my selfishness due to my various dalliances. Why was I unfaithful to my first wife? I have no idea. Jo decided that enough was enough and promptly told me that I would never see my two young children again. I went to the South of France to try to begin life once more.

'Who's this coming in the door?' cackled Stan, my friend I'd gone abroad with.

'I have no idea but I'd sure like to find out,' I replied with mirth in my voice. 'Check out the car she came in.'

Within 24 hours of meeting Jane, it seemed that she had 'sorted my life out'. I know it sounds crazy but really, gentle reader, she simply had. She replaced the cloudy road with new vision and clarity. Little did I know that years later she would become a psychologist.

In 1980, December of that year to be exact, Jane and I were living with her mum above the 'shop', a banqueting business that her mother owned, when I received a rather challenging and life-changing phone call. It was about 10 o'clock on a Sunday evening. We were watching a television programme that wasn't particularly holding our interest when the phone jangled. Looking forward to the diversion, I answered it.

'Hello, who's calling?'

'Iiiis that Davide?' a French woman asked on the other end.

'Yes it is; how can I help you?'

'I am ze neighbour of Josette here in France and I 'ave to tell you zat she 'as been taken to hopital for ze crazy people because she tried to kiiiilll 'erself wiz a shotgun. Ze little ones saw zis and were taken into my care zis afternoon. I 'ave to tell you, Davide, zat iiiif you don't pick zem up very fast, zen ze local council will tak zem into care.'

I told Jane that I would have to drive down to Bordeaux straight away to pick them up. What a bombshell that was for her. Firstly, she had never been a mother before, and secondly, I don't remember ever asking her if she would come with me, not to mention thirdly, I didn't consider for a second what she might be giving up. I just expected her to understand and jump to this new tune that had arrived in our lives.

We didn't even load up the car. We didn't have time. We just literally put our coats on and drove as fast as we could to Dover, then across 'Le Manche', and on down to Bordeaux, arriving the following afternoon.

When we arrived we found two frightened children almost cowering in the corner. They had very few clothes with them: just what they were standing up in, and one other piece each. No toys, just tears accompanied their tired little faces. Forlorn and forgotten they walked out of their 'home', and clambered into the car. I don't even want to discuss the situation that Jo was in at this time in the mental institution she had been committed to, or the cruelty she had to endure during her life, from the man she had chosen to spend her life with. Suffice it to say, the children were completely and utterly lost and abandoned by those that should have loved them. Jane had to adjust pretty quickly to her new found 'family'.

I remember that it was raining profusely, on the way back to dear old Blighty. Cats and dogs you might say. I had to get out of the car at one point to sort something out with one of the lights. I recall very vividly that I was feeling intensely hot; as if I had a fever. In fact I was 'burning up', so getting out of the car in the pouring rain felt wonderful. The fever continued unabated the entire journey back to London. This meant that Jane had to drive, and try her best to comfort the traumatised little ones in the back. I was getting to the stage of being in serious trouble health wise. That is about all I remember about the journey, as I slept most of the way back. When Jane had finally got us all home, she called the doctor who came very quickly. He diagnosed pleurisy and I was sent to the hospital for a chest X-ray, late that very night.

'He must have 6 weeks of complete bed rest,' the doctor told Jane, 'He can't do anything as this infection is quite dangerous and we must monitor it carefully.'

There you are then, my friend. Jane, not yet my wife (I hadn't asked her at this point), has her boyfriend in bed, seriously ill, two children who don't know her from a bowl of fruit and a job to do, on top of all that, to keep the wolf from the door, so to speak. I couldn't work, I was 'signed off' for 6 weeks. The clients for the taxi I had been driving for a living would have to find someone else. (I was, at the time, 'resting' from my career as an actor.) If that ain't love then I don't know what is. Real love is a verb, a doing word, and needs action to make it work.

In 1991, Jane was living alone in England with the four children (by this time we had two children of our own) as I was working in Frankfurt in Germany in a show called *A Slice of Saturday Night*. At home, we had neighbours to the left of us and neighbours to the right. The left-hand neighbours were a wonderful couple, however, the neighbours to the right left a lot to be desired, in fact they were horrible. There were loads of them living in a tiny house. They complained about anything and everything whenever they could. It seemed like they were on the planet to make everyone's life a misery. They so needed Jesus in their lives. Jane and I couldn't bring the Lord's love to them because I wasn't following Him and Jane didn't know Him. Anyway, I digress again. (How many times have I digressed in this book? Have you been counting? That many?) One morning there was a knock on the door. Remember, at this point I was in Germany and was not there to be the 'protector'. Jane answered it to find a very irate neighbour standing there in curlers and dressing gown, a woodbine dangling from her cracked lips. She began to berate Jane using all the expletives she knew. Jane finally asked her to come to the point. The woman next door told Jane in no uncertain terms that the noise from her alarm clock had woken her poor husband from his slumber this morning, and if that happened again then… (I'm afraid I can't repeat what she said would come to pass but I think you get the picture).

That morning, gentle reader, Jane made a momentous decision. She would be putting the house on the market forthwith, with or without my permission.

'I have no problem with that,' I told her later that day when she phoned me.

It was at this point that Jane turned her face heavenward and threw up a challenge to Almighty God. 'If You are really there, and David suggests You are, then I need proof. You know the situation we are in, living next door to this family. I can't stand it any longer. You need to do something and quickly. If You do then I'll believe in You and I'll follow You for the rest of my life.'

I really think that God loves a challenge now and again.

Later that day Jane began the arduous task of finding another property. Meanwhile, I was still in Germany pirouetting on a stage in Frankfurt.

I remember quite vividly one day phoning home to hear Jane saying, 'I have to go and see three houses that look very interesting. If you could fly home on Monday for 24 hours, you could see them with me.'

I immediately booked the flights and duly arrived on Monday morning in Jane's office in Romford. She showed me the details of the properties. Just one stuck out as far as I was concerned.

'That's the one, Janie,' I cried enthusiastically. 'Let's see that one today!'

'We can't see that one till Wednesday, David, and you'll be back in Frankfurt by then.'

'Give me the phone. I'll call the agent now.' I dialled the number, 'Hello. Can I speak to the person dealing with C17905 please?' I waited. I waited some more. I could hear elevator music playing in the background, how annoying. Finally someone spoke.

'Hello, can I help you?'

'I would like to view C17905 please.'

'I'm afraid that won't be possible until Wednesday, sir.'

'Do you wish to sell that property or would you like to sit on it for another 6 months?' I asked, trying very hard to keep the frustration out of my voice.

'Yes of course, sir,' replied the gentle man on the other end of the phone.

'Then be at the house at 2 p.m. today and you have half a chance of selling it to me.'

We were at the property at 1:30 so we could have a little 'squiz round' on our own. From the outside, we could immediately see the potential it had. We were quite excited actually, so by the time the estate agent showed up I was positively bubbling over with enthusiasm.

'What do you think, sir?' the agent asked, after I had whipped round the place in 5 minutes flat.

'We'll give you seventy grand for the house,' I said straight away.

'No we won't, David!' retorted Jane, 'We'll give you sixty-eight grand and not a penny more.'

'I'll take that to the vendors and see if they will accept that offer.'

Jane heard from the estate agent about a week later.

'Mrs Aldous? Your offer has been accepted by the vendors.'

I had been back in Germany nearly a month. I had been asking Jane practically every time I phoned her whether she had heard from the estate agent regarding the house. What was happening? Did they want us to sign papers? Questions, questions, questions. Every time she always replied the same way.

'I've given this to God, David. It's nothing to do with me at all.'

At this point, we were still yet to pay any money at all. Nothing! Nada! Not a bean! Actually, I was beginning to wonder if we had secured the house in any way. I just took it that it might have been sold to someone else.

One day while on the phone to Jane, she informed me that she had been advised to proceed with the purchase on her own, in her name. *OK*, I thought, *why not? I'm not there to sign any papers, if it will speed the process up, then that's fine with me.*

I came back to England at the end of January 1991. I had missed the family very much indeed. It was so good to see them all. When I had seen my youngest daughter Lauren at Christmas time, she had been very angry with me: I had disappeared from her life as far as she was concerned. She was just 3 years old. So it was a relief to be home finally.

Two months later in the middle of March, Jane heard from her solicitor who told her that they were ready to sign and exchange contracts. The lawyer went on to explain, 'You will need to bring your cheque for the deposit.'

'How much will that be?' Jane asked.

'We will need a cheque for £2,315.25.'

I was flummoxed: 'How on earth are we going to find that then Jane?'

'I have absolutely no idea at all,' she replied without a solitary care in the world.

'I know, ask your dad, he'll stump up the dosh.'

'No David, you ask your father. No actually, on second thoughts, don't. It is now up to God to sort this one out,' she responded sceptically.

I will never forget that day. It was a Wednesday. I realised, perhaps for the first time, that I too was desperate to move to this wonderful new house.

'When do you have to take the cheque to the solicitor?' I asked Jane.

'On Friday morning.'

The day for exchange on our new house had finally arrived. I remember watching Jane walk down the stairs that morning dressed in a business suit, while I was eating my breakfast. I was thinking, *Where on earth is she going?*

'Why are you dressed like that, love?'

'I'm going to see the solicitor,' she replied quietly.

'And what are we going to do for money then?'

'I'm going to have to tell her that we can't proceed with the deal.'

I was so upset that this house was going to fall through. I remember as though it were yesterday. *What sort of witness is this? Why would God let us down at the last minute?* Jane walked to the door, she clutched her handbag from the hallstand and left.

I remember getting up and watching her: she walked down the tiny drive towards the car. Suddenly the postman appeared. He handed Jane a pile of letters. She walked back to the house with the mail in her right hand. For some reason she decided that perhaps she would look through the mail before going. 'Just in case,' she told me laughing at the very thought.

Jane stood in the doorway sorting through the letters passing me some bills and a letter. I opened it straight away and found a cheque inside.

'Jane!' I shouted at the top of my voice. 'I think you'd better take a look at this.'

Inside the letter was a cheque for £2,315.35. To this day, we are certain the solicitor made a mistake in her calculations, as we had 10p change. The tears fell that day. It was a day that changed Jane's life for ever. That day she started a journey that culminated in giving her life completely and totally to the Lord Jesus Christ some months later. God had not let us down. More than that, He had not let Jane down. He proved His love for her in such a real and personal way. Moreover, as I write this, we still live in that same house, glory to God.

CHAPTER 12

THEN WILL I HEAR FROM HEAVEN

Do you forgive easily? Do you find it easy to forgive someone who hurts you? Are you holding any resentment against anyone today? I believe that forgiveness is a key factor to God's love shining through and being made manifest in our lives. I have always found it very easy to forgive, anyone. I never thought that this would ever be a problem in my life. I have a heart that's open. Why? Because as an actor (which I was for 25 years) I needed to be in touch with my emotions. What better way to be in touch than to feel them? So whenever they were displayed on screen or stage, to the casual viewer, they would seem real and believable. That surely is the actor's job – to make the character come to life and to breathe. But this is fraught with problems, too. A person who subscribes to this philosophy can and will be hurt often in their lives. However, having said that, there is real benefit to having such a warm and open heart. You are always able to feel when someone loves you. You can sense very powerfully what someone thinks of you. Not only that, but your feelings radiate from you as well. After what I have described in this book to you so far, I feel that because of my 'open heart', the love I always knew I had is pouring out of me in such a real way. All I can tell you is it is wonderful, an amazing gift and blessing from my Father in heaven. I'm sure you feel this love right now as you read this book.

Forgiveness then, is a precursor to love. It needs to be resident inside you. Jesus was very outspoken on this issue when He said in Matthew 6:14, 'For if you forgive men when they sin against you, your heavenly Father will also forgive you.'

And again, later in the same book when Peter asks Jesus a very pointed question about forgiveness: 'Master, how many times do I forgive a brother or sister who hurts me? Seven?' (Matthew 18:21, *The Message*).

What a response Jesus has to this interesting question. He immediately tells Peter and the gathered people a story of the 'unmerciful servant':

Seven! Hardly. Try seventy times seven.

The kingdom of God is like a king who decided to square accounts with his servants. As he got under way, one servant was brought before him who had run up a debt of a hundred thousand dollars. He couldn't pay up, so the king ordered the man, along with his wife, children, and goods, to be auctioned off at the slave market.

The poor wretch threw himself at the king's feet and begged, 'Give me a chance and I'll pay it all back.' Touched by his plea, the king let him off, erasing the debt.

The servant was no sooner out of the room when he came upon one of his fellow servants who owed him ten dollars. He seized him by the throat and demanded, 'Pay up. Now!'

The poor wretch threw himself down and begged, 'Give me a chance and I'll pay it all back.' But he wouldn't do it. He had him arrested and put in jail until the debt was paid. When the other servants saw this going on, they were outraged and brought a detailed report to the king.

The king summoned the man and said, 'You evil servant! I forgave your entire debt when you begged me for mercy. Shouldn't you be compelled to be merciful to your fellow servant who asked for mercy?' The king was furious and put the screws to the man until he paid back his entire debt. And that's exactly what my Father in heaven is going to do to each one of you who doesn't forgive unconditionally anyone who asks for mercy.
(Matthew 18:22–35, *The Message*)

Corrie Ten Boom was a survivor of the terrible atrocities of the Holocaust. She lived in the Netherlands and was sent to a concentration camp for trying to save the lives of Jewish people who were still in the country during the Second World War. In 1947 she was preaching in Germany and told a story of personal forgiveness that is very eloquently described in her book *Tramp for The Lord*. At the end of this service where she had brought God's word on forgiveness, and while at the back of the meeting shaking hands with everyone, she saw a man who had been one of the most brutal guards at the concentration camp 'Ravensbruck' where she had been incarcerated. He was approaching her to perhaps thank her for the word she had brought. Needless to say she was very reluctant to forgive him. However, as he approached, she gained the strength to pray to the Lord that He would help her in being able to forgive this person. She writes in her book that she was able to forgive him, and that, 'For a long moment we grasped each other's hands, the former guard and the former prisoner. I had never known God's love so intensely, as I did then.'

You see? Quite simply, she felt the power of God's love right there and then because she had forgiven totally. She had to do this with her will because emotion was not able to help her. Why? Well, she obviously had no reason to want to forgive what this man had done to her and her sister, who hadn't survived the camp. Therefore, she had to forgive him, after praying, with her will. 'I will forgive that man.'

'I will forgive my mum for what she did to me.'

'I will forgive my boss for how I was treated.'

'With my will, I will forgive.'

When that forgiveness comes, then the love of God can pour into your life in this wonderful and powerful way.

I was in Israel recently guiding a tour of the Holy Land on a coach. Each morning I would greet the intrepid explorers, and bring them a word from the Lord. This word could be quite short or long, depending on where we were going that day. One day as we journeyed toward the historic Dead Sea and Masada, I brought a word to them on God's love and His forgiveness. I told the gathered pilgrims that love was all that really mattered in our walk with the Lord Jesus Christ, because if we actually got that right, then all the other factors would fall into place. If we loved our fellow man as Jesus loved us, then how can we fail? I went on to say that the churches are full of people that won't love the way our Lord demands. 'Perhaps,' I mused, 'this is the reason that "Revival" has not come to our land. Are we ready to accept the poor, the downtrodden, the dispossessed, the homeless, the drug addict, the prostitute into the warm pews that we inhabit week after week?'

I went on to discuss at length the Sermon on the Mount (Matthew 5 to 7). If your Bible has headings, it makes life much easier to pinpoint the issues Jesus talked about in that incredible sermon. I often wonder what it must have been like to sit at the feet of our Lord, as He brought such wonderful understanding to who His Father was: revealing His heart to all who would listen. I read Matthew 5:38–42 to my valiant listeners. This is taken from *The Message*:

Here's another old saying that deserves a second look: 'Eye for eye, tooth for tooth.' Is that going to get us anywhere? Here's what I propose: 'Don't hit back at all.' If someone strikes you, stand there and take it. If someone drags you into court and sues for the shirt off your back, gift-wrap your best coat and make a present of it. And if someone takes unfair advantage of you, use the occasion to practice the servant life. No more tit-for-tat stuff. Live generously.

Awesome words from the Lord.

I also discussed at some length the Lord's prayer. This was the way the Lord taught us to pray. Someone just asked Him face to face in a matter of fact way: 'Lord, how should we pray?' Jesus responded with such passion when He replied.

Our Father which art in heaven, Hallowed be thy name.
Thy kingdom come, Thy will be done in earth, as it is in heaven.
Give us this day our daily bread.
And forgive us our debts, as we forgive our debtors.

And lead us not into temptation, but deliver us from evil:
For thine is the kingdom, and the power, and the glory,
for ever. Amen.

(Matthew 6:9–13, KJV)

Jesus was teaching about love in a more than unusual way.
'Love your enemies' He said. *What do you mean 'love your
enemies'? I have enough trouble loving my friends, how can I start
loving people I don't like?* I went on to say that this is what is
required of us. We have to achieve this. How? Well, just as we
forgive with our will (remember Corrie Ten Boom? She
forgave with her will and the Lord responded powerfully), we
do the same with loving our enemies. All is tied up with
forgiveness. In the Lord's prayer we see, 'and forgive us our
debts, as we forgive our debtors.' Isn't it great the way the Lord
teaches us? If we would only follow His example and teaching
then all would be incredible. I finished by saying the following:

There is a tremendous attack on husbands, wives and children;
the very structure of the family is under constant attack.
Where does Satan attack us? In the very foundation of the
family: in love and forgiveness. If in our daily lives with our
families, we can't forgive each other and we can't see a way to
love one another, the structure of the unit falls apart. This is
Satan's ploy to break it down for good. To bring down the
walls of the family once and for all, for without it we are lost.

I then asked the gathered people on that coach to respond to God's powerful word. I asked them all to bow their heads and to close their eyes and to seek God for any un-forgiveness that was present in their hearts. I asked them to simply raise their hands in response to this 'altar call'. Out of the 51 people gathered on that coach, three quarters of them responded by raising their hands, and I was able to pray a prayer of release for them right there and then. Would you, gentle reader, take a break from reading this book to search your heart, for any un-forgiveness that may be lurking in the dark recesses of your heart that you are not aware of? Take this time to ask the Father. If you have any un-forgiveness, would you repeat a prayer that I will pray for you? If not then just skip to the next chapter. If you would like to pray this prayer then repeat it out loud, or in your heart, as you please, but repeat it with all of your heart and mind. Replace the dotted line with the name of the person you are praying for.

Lord Jesus, I come before You now in humility and obedience.

I ask You to help me forgive ....

With my will, I make this decision to release .... into Your hands and with my will, I forgive ....

Thank You, Holy Spirit. I ask now that Your love

would flow down on me in a supernatural way, that I would be consumed in You.

I ask You this in the name of Your wonderful Son, Jesus Christ, my Lord.

Amen.

CHAPTER 13

AND WILL BRING YOU BACK FROM CAPTIVITY

I have just finished my first television documentary called *Church Without Walls*. I want to share with you a little about the history of the making of this programme and God's favour in the process.

About 18 months ago, I was having a cup of tea with a friend of mine who cleans our house once a month. Terri was actually very instrumental in bringing me back to the Lord in 1991. That is why she is such a dear friend. She does lots of things to help people; in addition to cleaning houses, she is also an awesome hairdresser. Anyway, she was at home this particular day and we were sharing a few moments together before she got back to the grindstone of cleaning my house. I suddenly, and without realising, said to her, 'Terri, what is it you do on a Saturday morning? I remember you telling me some time ago but I've forgotten.'

She sipped her tea, pondered a little before answering, and replied, 'I help out making tea and chatting to the down and outs of Victoria in London. We start at around 7 a.m. and work until 9:30 a.m/10 a.m. It is so rewarding seeing the joy on the people's faces as we minister to them.'

'That is awesome. I'm really glad you get blessed by doing that. I can tell you I could never do it. It doesn't float my boat at all, I have to say.'

Terri went on, 'We have praise and worship around a tree first of all at about 6:30 a.m. We worship God and sometimes the guys will join in, too.'

Praise and worship around a tree in Victoria, eh? My mind was working overtime at this point. *This would make such a good documentary.*

'Who is the pastor, Terri?'

'A wonderful man of God called Kurt Erickson,' replied Terri. 'Why?'

'I think this would make an incredible film. What do you think?'

'Well, it depends. These men and women on the streets are not ones to want to glorify their predicament. Some of them may not like it at all. Some of the people we serve are on the run from the police or loved ones and simply don't want to be found, so we have to be very mindful of their wishes. I hope you can understand and appreciate that, David.'

'That goes without saying,' I murmured. 'Can I phone Kurt and find out how he feels about this?'

'Of course, here's his number. You'll probably get him on Monday morning.'

I could hardly wait. I was really excited about the possibility of making a documentary: my first.

'Kurt, good morning to you, sir. My name is David Aldous, I'm a friend of Terri's and I was talking to her on Saturday. I was wondering if I could run something by you regarding your ministry on Saturday mornings. What do you call it by the way?'

'Church without walls,' was his immediate reply.

What a great name: a church that didn't have any walls. Exactly what church is supposed to be. 'Church' in the Greek is 'ecclesia', which means 'people'.

'I was wondering if we could meet up at all in the next week or so? I don't know how your schedule is looking at the moment?'

'What would this be about, David?' Kurt's American brogue coming down the telephone wire.

'I was wondering if I could discuss the possibility of making a documentary about your work with the poor, dispossessed, drug addicts etc.?'

'Wow! OK! Yes, then I guess we should meet. Would you be free on Friday at about 1:30 p.m.? We could meet at Starbucks in Victoria and have a coffee.'

We met as arranged. Kurt showed me where 'the tree' was. I told him that I was fascinated by the thought of having praise and worship round a tree on a Saturday morning.

'Sometimes the presence of the Holy Spirit is almost tangible, David,' Kurt told me. 'We are always blessed by what happens here in the presence of the Lord.'

I can't wait, I thought to myself. *When can I get started?*

'When would be a good time to come and see the work you do, Kurt?'

'Well, what about tomorrow morning? Bright and early at 6:30 a.m.? How does that sound?'

It sounds really early to me my friend, I said to myself.

'That sounds great, Kurt. I'll be here with some crew tomorrow morning at 6:30 a.m.'

Do you *know* what 6:30 a.m. is like for someone who doesn't do early mornings? Well, I felt like it was way too early to be moving around. When I was acting in TV shows and different films I've been in, I had earlier mornings than this but I had forgotten what it was like. I love to wake up when I wake up. My friend Martin came with me as he was going to be in charge of sound on this project. He knocked on my door at 5 a.m. With my dogs barking at the top of their voices, the whole house was woken up.

We arrived at the location at around 6:10 a.m. or thereabouts. It was still dark for goodness' sake – we couldn't see anyone or anything. Through the darkness, however, we did see the ministry team arriving: setting up the urn, getting the cups out, preparing for whoever would turn up that morning. Lots of hustle and bustle. It was an awesome time, really it was. I looked at what was going on and could almost see the entire film unfolding before my eyes. I was hoping against all hope that the people who were being served wouldn't have a problem with us filming. We told Kurt that we would only use small equipment, the sort of camera equipment that news crews would use. This was so the 'stars' of the show wouldn't feel intimidated. That was very important for me and for Kurt, too. I explained to Kurt that I would need to make sure that everyone we featured on film would be happy with this and that if not then we wouldn't show their faces: we would digitally disguise their features. Kurt had already spoken to quite a few people before we even got there because we were expected.

We made the decision that we would begin filming next Saturday and carry on for two subsequent weekends after that. I resolved that I would be financing this film myself. Why? Only the Lord knew. I had no idea.

Early the following Saturday, I was awake and busy at 4:30 a.m. to leave the house at 5 a.m. My sound man, Martin Jordan, was meeting me at 5 o'clock. He looked as if he'd never seen that time before either. My daughter, Jemma, was going to be camera assistant on this shoot, so it was a learning curve for all of us. I gave the 'team' instructions, that if anything moved 'shoot it'. If we didn't have it in the 'can', then it could never be included in the final film. As an aside at this point, when we had finished shooting all the footage, I noted that we had filmed 7.5 hours altogether. I thought that was a lot for a 30-minute documentary. However, since then I have been reliably informed that actually that is about the correct ratio. Another of the Lord's blessings! There were to be many before this film had been finished.

We set off not knowing exactly what we would find, or whether we would be accepted by the men and women we were going to capture on film. I was after testimonies of people who had had their lives changed by the power of the living Christ – those who were now 'on fire' and serving God in a passionate way, with compassion driving them toward the goal the Lord had set. I knew that Kurt would be a real force during this film. I had already made some important decisions. I determined that I would shoot a 'formal interview' with this wonderful man of God. His passion was so consuming that I knew it would come over well on camera. What I didn't expect was the extent of God's grace through the interview.

The team began worshipping around the tree soon after 6:30 a.m. It was cold, so very cold, that November morning of 2005, not that you would have noticed from the wonderful sounds emanating from Victoria. They were in fine voice to a man with a guitarist who played his instrument powerfully and 'led' the worship. We set up and began filming all we could. The people gathered didn't seem to have a problem at all with what we were doing.

'Try to get closer, Jemma,' I encouraged. 'You are too far back. Think of the shot. Think of what you are trying to say to your audience as you line up the shot.'

We were always looking for the best angles we could get. On that first morning, I distinctly remember getting some footage of a man who was very very cold, sitting in a cardboard box of sorts – he was being fed tea by one of the team. It was so moving. Maria had so much compassion as she 'fed' him. I felt that this was exactly what Jesus would have done in this situation. Matthew 25:40 says this: 'The King will reply, "I tell you the truth, whatever you did for one of the least of these brothers of mine, you did for me."'

I marvel at the handiwork of the Lord's servants, as they tirelessly go about their devotion to their calling with such love and tenderness. This, then, was what this film was going to be about. Christ's love, and the love He implants in His 'workers': His awe-inspiring compassion.

I sat under the tree and began talking to 'Mark', that is what I shall call him for the sake of anonymity. He talked about how he loves to come to see Kurt and his ministry team every Saturday, and of how Kurt had helped him in lots of different sociological ways. Mark was about 60 years old, from Scotland, with a rugged complexion giving the impression of having spent a good deal of his life living 'rough' on the streets. He had spent a lot of time in Belfast and had certainly lived an interesting life. When we were ready to 'roll the camera', I asked him the pointed question, 'Anyway, tell me how you found Jesus round this tree?'

His answer was confusing, slightly off the point, maybe a little slurred in how he communicated. However, having said that, he finished with words that would deeply affect what I felt and how the film would be shaped. He said quite simply, 'Now that I've found Jesus, I'll never let Him go.' To me that encapsulated the entire ethos of the documentary after the first day of filming. That was God's purpose and His almighty grace in the situation. His favour was most definitely present.

We continued to shoot some wonderful footage. We also managed to do some other location work where we spoke to members of the general public as to what the church meant to them. The answers were quite unexpected in many ways. You really need to see the film to appreciate these responses.

The shooting continued for the next few Saturdays. We always managed to find some wonderful people to film.

I began to assemble the footage for editing which I did myself in my office. We used various pieces of music which at the time I thought would be perfect for the film. However, I had forgotten about the wonderfully murky world of 'clearing copyright'. To put it another way, one can't simply use someone's music and performance without paying for it. I tried to clear the copyright to use the music for the film but to no avail. *Where are you in this, Lord?* I thought in a moment of frustration.

At this point in the proceedings I need to cut to another story of God's incredible grace and favour in my life, and to jump back to 1995. You will understand very soon, after the next chapter.

CHAPTER 14

YOU WILL GO OUT IN JOY
AND BE LED FORTH IN PEACE

'You need to go to this conference, David,' said Kit, a really good friend and a partner in a drama group we ran at church.

'I don't want to go. You go!' I replied with a little venom in my voice. We had been at this discussion for about 20 minutes and were getting nowhere. To call it a 'discussion' would be a slight distortion as voices were definitely raised.

'I don't have the time to go all the way to Switzerland. I'm so busy next week, Kit, surely you can take some time off and go yourself?'

We both felt it was important that one of us should go to the CEVMA (Christian European Video Media Association) conference, as we had made a very good contact regarding a project we had both been working on.

What you need to know, my friend, is that I hate, with an absolute passion, networking. I find it so difficult to do. Some people thrive on it. Me? It leaves me cold, in fact freezing. I could picture the scene. Me trying to say all the things one is supposed to say when introducing oneself. Yuk! *OK Lord*, I mused to myself, *He ain't going to go, so I suppose I'll have to.* I remembered at this point that I had just finished reading a great and very funny book by Adrian Plass (*The Sacred Diary of Adrian Plass Aged 37 3/4*) where he was asked to go carol singing with his church one Christmas. He really didn't want to go so he set a 'fleece' before the Lord saying, 'Lord, if a small man of four foot six dressed in full Napoleonic regalia turns up at my house at 9:30 p.m. tomorrow evening singing "Maybe it's because I'm a Londoner", then I will know, Lord, that I am supposed to go carol singing.' (Incidentally, that is not a direct quote from the book, but you get the message.) Well I wasn't going to do that, but I did set a 'fleece' before Almighty God. I said to Him, 'Father, if You want me to go to this conference then I need someone to ring me up this afternoon and offer to pay for the flight and the cost of the conference. As You know, Lord, I have no money. That is the deal, take it or leave it, Father!'

At about 4:30 p.m. the telephone rang. A voice on the other end said, 'I believe I need to give you some money, David. The Lord has told me to offer you some money to pay for a flight and a conference.'

What can you say to that? *OK Lord, you win, I'll go.*

I arrived the following Friday and wasn't made to feel welcome at all. In fact, I felt very left out, completely isolated and alone. *Never mind, it'll get better.*

By the time worship was over the following morning, I was in no better a mood. I had lunch, alone!

'Lord, we need to talk. I need to tell You that if You don't tell me very very soon why I'm here, then I promise You, I'll be on tomorrow's flight back to London.' And I meant it.

I went to a seminar on 'Storytelling in film' presented by someone called Bart Gavigan, who, I was assured, was someone quite important in the film industry. He started by asking his audience to go and see any film by the director Quentin Tarantino. *Why would I want to go and see a movie by someone who's whole ethos was to commit to film as much violence as the censors would allow him to get away with?*

'You need to understand his worldview,' Bart went on. 'He was brought up by his grandmother in New York and was a projectionist in her cinema by the time he was 11 years old. He showed pornographic and violent films all the time in that cinema at that young age. What do you think his worldview would be in that situation?'

I was stunned by the things Bart was saying. I was captivated, sold.

'If you look at his films, what you will immediately see is his genius as a storyteller and director. He is incredible.' Bart went on to explain how a story is told. His lecture was nothing short of brilliant. I was thinking at the end of the afternoon, 'I would love to meet him.'

Dinner time came that evening, and there was a seat on a long table where Bart and his wife Patricia and son Gabriel were seated. They were at one end of the table and me at the other, with about 10 people between us. Suddenly, he got up from where he was sitting and plonked himself right next to me.

'Hi there, I'm Bart Gavigan,' he declared.

'I'm David Aldous and I'm honoured to meet you.'

We talked all through dinner that night. Everyone got up from the table at the end of the meal and went off to a film showing. We were still sitting at the table chatting. The other people came back from watching the films. We were still there. Cocoa was served, and yes we were still there. In fact, we chatted until about 3 o'clock in the morning.

'I believe this was a God plan not a good plan that we met, David,' said Bart, finally lifting his slim frame from the chair.

'Me, too, Bart. I couldn't agree more.'

'I need to go to bed, I'm exhausted,' croaked Bart. 'We have been chatting for hours, I need my sleep.'

'So Father,' I prayed after he had gone, 'this was why You brought me to Switzerland.'

I didn't hear from Bart for about 6 months after that conference until one evening he rang me at home. 'David, lovely to talk to you. How would you like to go to Malawi with me?'

'Where on earth is Malawi?' I asked after getting over the shock of speaking to him.

'It's in East Africa. We are going next week to make a film about the life of Reinhard Bonnke. Are you in?'

On the flight to Malawi, Bart went on to explain that the Lord had told him to take me with him.

'Why?' I asked him.

'I have absolutely no idea, David. I'm doing this in obedience.'

Over the next 4 years, I travelled the length and breadth of the continent of Africa seeing some amazing things, being moved to tears, seeing children, gathered singing, filming the most beautiful of sunsets I have ever witnessed. I even went to the USA with the team in the making of the film. It was only when making *Church without Walls* that I realised what the Lord had been doing. Through all that time I'd spent with Bart, the Lord had been preparing me. Training me, even. My teacher happened to be one of the world's best scriptwriters and directors. What a training ground.

Chapter 15

Seek The Lord While He May Be Found, Call On Him While He Is Near

'Martin!' I said to my trusty sound man on the phone. 'We need to do a formal interview with Kurt for the film. You need to be on location in Canning Town on Sunday morning at 9 a.m. I really hope you can make it.'

'I just need to shift a few things round, but have no fear I will be there. I'll meet you at the location.'

My wife Jane was going to be coming on this particular shoot as a production assistant, meaning that she would carefully take down information to aid me in the edit. In other words, she would write down time codes and look at camera angles because we were only using two cameras and we really needed four. She was invaluable in the process. Jemma was there, too, working as camera operator. It was quite manic really as we were 'shooting' this sequence in a very small flat in Canning Town, and there was barely enough room to swing a cat, so to speak.

I won't bore you with all the details of the shoot. Suffice it to say that what emerged was a story of passion, compassion and love in a hurting world: a story of one man's tenacity in bringing someone who clearly needed God, into His family. It was wonderful to listen to. Kurt told me about someone named 'Kenny' who from an early age had suffered from a stroke and found himself on the street. He had been brought up in foster care. He had never had a family to speak of. When Kurt met Kenny in a park he tried to persuade him to come to a home group meeting, but to no avail. Kenny wasn't having any of it: not interested at all. 'Get away from me!' he yelled at Kurt.

I'm not going to tell you all that happened just in case you would like to see the film. However, the result was that after 4 years of persuasion and prayer, Kenny gave his heart to the Lord Jesus Christ, and became a completely new man. The story along the way though is fascinating. If you would like to see the film, then it is available, and I will give you the address and telephone number of where you can purchase it at the end of this book. During the making of this film, it was always my intention to sell it on licence to TV companies, to launch me onto the unsuspecting world as a filmmaker. How naive was that then, eh? The Lord clearly had other plans. The fact is that when it was entered into various competitions, it never won. It was highly recommended, but it didn't win. It was up against £3 million budget films from the BBC, for example. God's plan was simple. To be able to show to people in small gatherings, conferences etc., the work of Eleos Christian Church: the love and compassion they have for the ministry they are engaged in. This was in order to raise money for their work by selling the DVD, so that they could continue in the work God has clearly called them to do. What an honour to be used by God in such a wonderful way.

A little after this time, I had compiled what is known as a 'rough cut' – the programme in its raw state – to see if the pictures worked as they were assembled (it's also sometimes known as an 'off-line edit'). I sent the film to my pastor, Chris Demitriou, who also had contacts in the television world, to see what he thought. He came back with quite a few suggestions, all of which I heeded and worked on. One of the ideas Chris came up with was to make the film a Christmas film. I thought about this and then, after making the decision to adapt the film to accommodate this idea, the blessings began to flow once more. We filmed *Church Without Walls* on Christmas Eve morning, where the 'clients' received gifts from the people of Kurt's ministry. We went out for a night shoot to film homeless people on the street that very evening. It was so powerful.

One Sunday a few weeks later, we were driving home from church when I suddenly cried at the top of my voice, 'Silent night! Write that down quickly, "Silent Night"!'

The Lord was giving me an entire arrangement for this song on the journey home. I heard it as clearly as if I were listening to a CD. I also knew my daughter Lauren was supposed to sing it. It would appear at the end of the film. I immediately called my wonderful friend Jerry, who had already done some of the music to the film, to tell him what I wanted for this end piece of music.

Jerry is not a Christian, but has on a number of occasions done various pieces of music for me. We have been friends for many many years. I love him like a brother. Actually, as you are reading this book, it would be wonderful if you could just spend a few minutes praying for Jerry, for his salvation, for if he came to know Jesus as his Lord and Saviour, what a blessing he would be for the Body of Christ. I digress. (You have probably noticed already, gentle reader, I do that a lot.) I arranged with Jerry to pop over to the studio to begin working on this arrangement the very next morning. What a fantastic blessing it was. The song was recorded in no time at all and sounded exactly as I had heard it in my head. *Wonderful. Thank You Jesus, thank you Jerry Chapman.* So now the film was really taking on a Christmas feel.

'The copyright clearance still hasn't come through,' I complained. 'I think I'm going to have to re-edit the film and remove all the music I can't use.' I was talking to Martin, trying to make a decision as to what to do.

'I don't think you have a choice really, David,' Martin replied. 'That means I will have to do a completely new sound mix. What music are you going to use?'

That was a very good question. Enter Bart Gavigan. A few months earlier, Bart had seen the film when I showed it to him at a family party. He watched and watched, tears filling his eyes as the film drew to a close.

'I don't know what to say, David. I'm at a loss for words. This film is world class. If I had to mark it in an exam I would give it B+ at the moment. But with three small changes it would be A+.' Bart went on to tell me the changes that needed to be made. (Actually all the changes needed were contained in the end credits.) He went on to say, 'David, it feels to me like I have just looked at a beautiful picture my son has done. He has shown me what he has done and I'm so proud. Now I know why you came to Africa with me, for such a time as this.'

'Bart, this is David,' I said deep into the recesses of the phone, 'I was wondering if you could help me with the film?'

'What seems to be the problem?'

'I can't clear the copyright on the music I am using. I have tried for months now to get the music cleared, but the music company isn't even answering my phone calls and emails.'

'Well!' retorted Bart, after what seemed an eternity, 'I did tell you that it was going to be a veritable minefield you were going to enter when you have to try to clear copyright. However, I might have some music here in my library that I own the copyright to that you could use if you wanted.' *Praise God*, I thought to myself. I had already resigned myself to the fact that a re-edit was inevitable. I was looking at days and days of work, as was Martin. Hey ho, these things are sent to try us.

Within a few days I had picked up the music from Bart and was looking to see if anything was suitable. There were two pieces that I decided on. These were placed in the film and they worked amazingly well. Hallelujah. There was still a gaping hole to fill though. I needed 5 minutes and 37 seconds' worth of awe-inspiring music to fill the middle. It had to be exact, too. *Well Lord?* I pondered.

'Jerry!' I pleaded to my friend the next evening on the phone. 'Do you think, under any circumstance, that I could prevail on you to, errr… help me out of a little tight spot I've got myself in?'

'Here we go, David, what is it you want now?'

'Well there's a tiny hole in the middle of the film that needs filling with superb music.'

'What do you need?' replied Jerry sounding quite concerned.

'I need exactly 5 minutes and 37 seconds of music to be written in the key of E minor. It needs to be a solo violin with a full orchestra backing and I need it yesterday.'

That was Friday evening. By Saturday evening Jerry called me to say he had done the music to my exact specifications. I picked it up that same evening and put the music into the film. It was nothing short of a miracle. The music fit absolutely perfectly. Not only that, there is one point in the film where I make a joke with Kurt about getting up so early in the morning and the music Jerry had written changed pace exactly at that moment to reflect this. It was as though Jerry was watching the film as he composed the music, which he wasn't, as he hadn't even seen the film. Jesus was certainly on His throne. I think for me to tell you all the blessings we as a crew received from making this film, I would have to devote an entire book to that one thing. (I may do that one day.) Suffice it to say that this process taught me so much about God's love and compassion for His people. Seeing those less fortunate than you really makes you think. It changes your perception of who God is, and what He thinks are the important issues in our lives. I found this a mind-changing experience: I was being changed from glory into glory all through this.

Chapter 16

Perfect Love Drives Out Fear

O love that will not let me go,
I rest my weary soul in thee;
I give thee back the life I owe,
That in thine ocean depths its flow
May richer, fuller be.

O light that followest all my way,
I yield my flickering torch to thee:
My heart restores its borrowed ray,
That in thy sunshine's blaze its day
May brighter, fairer be.

O joy that seekest me through pain,
I cannot close my heart to thee:
I trace the rainbow through the rain,
And feel the promise is not vain,
That morn shall tearless be.
(George Matheson, 1882)

I have felt love like this when I watched my beautiful children being born: to see their faces for the first time. The way they screw up their little features as they wait dependently on you to feed them, to love them, to look after them, to care for them. Never do they have any doubt that you will hurt them or harm them. Never do they mistrust you or think that you don't love them. They have total faith in you as a parent. That is something of how God looks on us, as His children. Imagine then when He sees one of His precious little ones straying off the path He had set for them. How He must allow the tears to fall for the lost. How He tries to bring back the broken-hearted and the poor of spirit. How can we help Him? We can aid the Father by paying attention to His voice. By listening to what He would have us do for Him. You have started this journey by hearing God's word. Even through reading this book, your journey into this new and exciting life has begun. What are you going to do with that information? How will you respond? Will you make a conscious decision to change your life to that which God will reveal to you? Will you dedicate your entire life to Him? Will you promise to follow the Lord wherever He may lead? This, friend, is a total commitment to God and His almighty service. It's exciting. You never know where it is going to lead you. This love that you are now feeling needs to be shared. You need to go out and let others partake of this awesome love you feel right now. Let the

Holy Spirit guide you as to where you must take this, with whom it must be shared. He will tell you, I promise you that, if you listen and hearken to His voice. Over the past months, I have learned to 'Go where the peace is'. Wherever you find that peace is where you will find God, in any given situation.

A very good friend of mine, Canon Andrew White, is the Archbishop of Canterbury's special envoy to the Middle East. He is one of the most renowned hostage negotiators in the Middle East. He has done amazing work, and continues to battle tirelessly for peace in that region. He will tell you that in the midst of war, devastation and destruction, God is at work. He says that even in his church of St George's in Baghdad, the glory of God falls all the time. He is so blessed to be working there in Iraq. The stories he has are awesome in their own right. It is all about God loving us and us loving the Father right back. I love the Lord now so much that it is too difficult to put into words. I find myself at the strangest of times just praising Him for who He is and what He has accomplished in my life.

As I now reflect on the birth of my beloved children, a tear forms in the corner of my eye, for such is the unconditional love I have for my little ones. They are not so little now, they have all grown up and two of them have children of their own. My daughter Natasha tells me that when my grandson, Sammy, was born, for the first time in her life she understood the power of this love. For her, this was maternal love. For God, it is all love, all-consuming love, and if we allow Him to He will burn all the dross away in our lives and reveal the real us: who we really are.

It was very recently that I found out for the first time who I really was, what I was like, who I was as a person and why God loved me so much. When I met the real me, there were lots of tears. I was happy to see, that there, underneath all the veneer and polish, was this person God had made, and I liked what I saw. I have learned that on this journey, you need to like yourself, really like yourself for who and what you are, and moreover what God has created.

In his letter to the church in Rome, Paul the Apostle says very eloquently:

Love from the center of who you are; don't fake it. Run for dear life from evil; hold on for dear life to good. Be good friends who love deeply; practice playing second fiddle.

Don't burn out; keep yourselves fueled and aflame. Be alert servants of the Master, cheerfully expectant. Don't quit in hard times; pray all the harder. Help needy Christians; be inventive in hospitality.
(Romans 12:9, *The Message*)

And again, in verse 20, Paul writes:

> Our Scriptures tell us that if you see your enemy hungry, go buy that person lunch, or if he's thirsty, get him a drink. Your generosity will surprise him with goodness. Don't let evil get the best of you; get the best of evil by doing good.

Would you allow me to pray for you? Would you repeat a simple prayer as we finish this time together? Once again, wherever you see the dotted lines replace that with the name of the person you are bringing to prayer. During this prayer, you will be asking the Lord to impact friends and family, but you will have the opportunity to bring one specific person before the Lord. Before we do that, I wanted to let you know that the words spoken in the show of *O Love That Will Not Let Me Go* are included in this book in the final chapter. That is so that you can look at the scriptures any time you like. When you are feeling down, when you are thinking that the world does not understand you, when you think that the end of the world is happening around you and you can't feel peace, then know this: your loving heavenly Father is there for you. Your comforter, the Holy Spirit, is interceding for you (praying to the Father on your behalf) and Jesus your Saviour is loving you so much – all the scriptures that prove this will be on hand for you at any time to bring you comfort and solace. Know this also, that I love you for the step you have taken, and may the blessings of Almighty God be with you now and for ever more. May His Almighty love follow you day by day. May the Lord bless you and keep you. May the light of His countenance give you peace now and always, world without end. Amen.

Repeat this prayer with me:

Heavenly Father, I love You now more than I could ever imagine or believe. I give You the praise and honour due Your name for this miracle that is happening in my life right now. I pray in the mighty name of Your Son Jesus Christ of Nazareth that You would continue the work You have done in my life. I pray, Lord, that I would be effective in bringing this love I feel to other people around me, friends and family. Right now though Jesus I want to pray specifically for .... who needs the impact of this love right at this moment. I pray that ....'s life is changed completely and that You begin a real work.

You are glorious and wonderful Father, and I love You from the core of my being. I promise to follow Your footsteps for the rest of my life. In the name of Jesus, Your Son, I pray.

Amen and Amen.

For more information and to purchase a copy of the documentary *Church Without Walls* please write to:

Eleos Christian Church
204a Cambridge Heath Road
Bethnal Green
London E2 9NQ
020 7366 4472

David Aldous can be contacted at:
davidaldous@blueyonder.co.uk

Chapter 17

Words From The Show Of O Love That Will Not Let Me Go

O love that will not let me go,
I rest my weary soul in thee;
I give thee back the life I owe,
That in thine ocean depths its flow
May richer, fuller be.

O light that followest all my way,
I yield my flickering torch to thee:
My heart restores its borrowed ray,
That in thy sunshine's blaze its day
May brighter, fairer be.

O joy that seekest me through pain,
I cannot close my heart to thee:
I trace the rainbow through the rain,
And feel the promise is not vain,
That morn shall tearless be.
(George Matheson, 1882)

God so loved the world, that He gave His only son.
That whosoever would believe in Him would have life everlasting.
(John 3:16, paraphrased)

Place me like a seal over your heart,
like a seal on your arm;
for love is as strong as death,
its jealousy unyielding as the grave.
It burns like a blazing fire,
like a mighty flame.
(Song of Songs 8:6)

Love is patient. Love is kind. It does not envy, it does not boast, it is not proud. It is not rude, it is not self-seeking, it is not easily angered, it keeps no record of wrongs. Love does not delight in evil but rejoices with the truth. It always protects, always trusts, always hopes, always perseveres.

Love never fails …

And now these three remain: faith, hope and love. But the greatest of these is love.
(1 Corinthians 13:4–8,13)

If anyone acknowledges that Jesus is the Son of God, God lives in him and he in God. And so we know and rely on the love God has for us.

(1 John 4:15,16)

As soon as Judas took the bread, Satan entered into him.

'What you are about to do, do quickly,' Jesus told him, but no one at the meal understood why Jesus said this to him. Since Judas had charge of the money, some thought Jesus was telling him to buy what was needed for the Feast, or to give something to the poor. As soon as Judas had taken the bread, he went out. And it was night.

When he was gone, Jesus said, 'Now is the Son of Man glorified and God is glorified in him. If God is glorified in him, God will glorify the Son in himself, and will glorify him at once.

'My children, I will be with you only a little longer. You will look for me, and just as I told the Jews, so I tell you now: Where I am going, you cannot come.

'A new command I give you: Love one another. As I have loved you, so you must love one another. By this all men will know that you are my disciples, if you love one another.'

Simon Peter asked him, 'Lord, where are you going?'

Jesus replied, 'Where I am going, you cannot follow now, but you will follow later.'

Peter asked, 'Lord, why can't I follow you now? I will lay down my life for you.'

Then Jesus answered, 'Will you really lay down your life for me? I tell you the truth, before the cock crows, you will disown me three times!'

(John 13:27–38)

Listen! My lover!
Look! Here he comes,
leaping across the mountains,
bounding over hills.
My lover is like a gazelle or a young stag.
Look! There he stands behind our wall,
gazing through the windows,
peering through the lattice.
My lover spoke and said to me,
'Arise, my darling,
my beautiful one, and come with me.
See! The winter is past;
the rains are over and gone.
Flowers appear on the earth;
the season of singing has come,
the cooing of doves is heard in our land.
The fig-tree forms its early fruit;
the blossoming vines spread their fragrance.

Arise, come, my darling;
my beautiful one, come with me.'
(Song of Songs 2:8–13)

How beautiful you are, my darling!
Oh, how beautiful!
Your eyes behind your veil are doves.
Your hair is like a flock of goats
descending from mount Gilead.
Your teeth are like a flock of sheep just shorn,
coming up from the washing.
Each has its twin;
not one of them is alone.
Your lips are like a scarlet ribbon
your mouth is lovely.
Your temples behind your veil
are like the halves of a pomegranate.
Your neck is like the tower of David,
built with elegance;
on it hang a thousand shields,
all of them shields of warriors.
(Song of Songs 4:1–4)

You have heard that it was said, 'Eye for eye, and tooth for tooth.' But I tell you, Do not resist an evil person. If someone strikes you on the right cheek, turn to him the other also. And if someone wants to sue you and take your tunic, let him have your cloak as well. If someone forces you to go one mile, go with him two miles. Give to the one who asks you, and do not turn away from the one who wants to borrow from you.

(Matthew 5:38–42)

Are not two sparrows sold for a penny? Yet not one of them will fall to the ground apart from the will of your Father. And even the very hairs of your head are all numbered. So don't be afraid; you are worth more than many sparrows.

(Matthew 10:29–31)

I'm saying my son, listen to my words, do not harden your heart for I am with you always, even to the end of the age.

My word will not return to me void but will come back to me bearing fruit.

Understand this, I am going to show you love such as you have never seen before. For I love you beyond your own finite mind.

For I am infinite.

Who shall separate us from the love of Christ? Shall trouble or hardship or persecution or famine or nakedness or danger or sword? As it is written:

'For your sake we face death all day long;

we are considered as sheep to be slaughtered.'

No, in all these things we are more than conquerors through him who loved us. For I am convinced that neither death nor life, neither angels nor demons, neither the present nor the future, nor any powers, neither height nor depth, nor anything else in all creation, will be able to separate us from the love of God that is in Christ Jesus our Lord.

(Romans 8:35–39)

'Lord, if you are willing, you can make me clean.'

Jesus reached out his hand and touched the man. 'I am willing,' he said. 'Be clean!' And immediately the leprosy left him.

(Luke 5:12–13)

He answered: '"Love the Lord your God with all your heart and with all your soul and with all your strength and with all your mind"; and, "Love your neighbour as yourself."'

(Luke 10:27)

Who is my neighbour?...

In the beginning was the Word, and the Word was with God, and the Word was God. He was with God in the beginning.

Through him all things were made; without him nothing was made that has been made. In him was life, and that life was the light of men. The light shines in the darkness, but the darkness has not understood it.

(John 1:1–5)

My command is this: Love each other as I have loved you. Greater love has no one than this, that he lay down his life for his friends.

(John 15:12,13)

How lovely is your dwelling place,
O LORD Almighty!
My soul yearns, even faints,
for the courts of the LORD;
my heart and my flesh cry out
for the living God.
Even the sparrow has found a home,
and the swallow a nest for herself,
where she may have her young –
a place near your altar,
O LORD Almighty, my King and my God.

Blessed are those who dwell in your house;
they are ever praising you.
(Psalm 84:1–4)

He who dwells in the shelter of the Most High
will rest in the shadow of the Almighty.
I will say of the LORD, 'He is my refuge and my fortress,
my God, in whom I trust' …
'Because he loves me,' says the LORD, 'I will rescue him;
I will protect him, for he acknowledges my name.
He will call upon me, and I will answer him;
I will be with him in trouble,
I will deliver him and honour him.
With long life will I satisfy him
and show him my salvation.'
(Psalm 91:1–2,14–16)

Dear friends, let us love one another, for love comes from God. Everyone who loves has been born of God and knows God. Whoever does not love does not know God, because God is love …

In this way, love is made complete among us so that we will have confidence on the day of judgment, because in this world we are like him. There is no fear in love. But perfect

love drives out fear, because fear has to do with punishment. The one who fears is not made perfect in love.
(1 John 4:7,8,17,18)

And hope does not disappoint us, because God has poured out his love into our hearts by the Holy Spirit, whom he has given us.
(Romans 5:5)

Love must be sincere. Hate what is evil; cling to what is good. Be devoted to one another in brotherly love. Honour one another above yourselves. Never be lacking in zeal, but keep your spiritual fervour, serving the Lord. Be joyful in hope, patient in affliction, faithful in prayer.
(Romans 12:9–12)

I will sing of your love and justice;
to you, O LORD, I will sing praise.
I will be careful to lead a blameless life –
when will you come to me?
(Psalm 101:1,2)

Here is love, vast as the ocean,
Loving kindness as a flood;
When the Prince of Life our ransom,
Shed for us His precious blood.
Who His love will not remember?
Who can cease to sing His praise?
He will never be forgotten,
Throughout Heav'n's eternal days.

On the mount of crucifixion,
Fountains opened deep and wide;
Through the floodgates of God's mercy
Flowed a vast and gracious tide;
Grace and love like mighty rivers
Poured incessant from above,
And Heav'n's peace and perfect justice
Kissed a guilty world in love.
(Robert S. Lowry and William Rees)

Praise the LORD, O my soul;
all my inmost being, praise his holy name.
Praise the LORD, O my soul,
and forget not all his benefits –
who forgives all your sins
and heals all your diseases,

who redeems your life from the pit
and crowns you with love and compassion,
who satisfies your desires with good things
so that your youth is renewed like the eagle's.
(Psalm 103:1–5)

Keep on loving each other as brothers. Do not forget to
entertain strangers, for by so doing some people have
entertained angels without knowing it. Remember those in
prison as if you were their fellow prisoners, and those who
are ill-treated as if you yourselves were suffering.
(Hebrews 13:1–3)

How deep the Father's love for us,
How vast beyond all measure,
That He should give His only Son
And make a wretch His treasure.
How great the pain of searing loss –
The Father turns His face away,
As wounds which mar the Chosen One
Bring many sons to glory.

Behold the man upon the cross,
My sin upon His shoulders;
Ashamed, I hear my mocking voice

Call out among the scoffers.
It was my sin that held Him there
Until it was accomplished;
His dying breath has brought me life –
I know that it is finished.

I will not boast in anything,
No gifts, no power, no wisdom,
But I will boast in Jesus Christ,
His death and resurrection.
Why should I gain from His reward?
I cannot give an answer;
But this I know with all my heart –
His wounds have paid my ransom.

Why should I gain from His reward?
I cannot give an answer;
But this I know with all my heart –
His wounds have paid my ransom.
('How Deep The Father's Love' by Stuart Townend
Copyright © 1995 Thankyou Music)

When they had finished eating, Jesus said to Simon Peter,
'Simon son of John, do you truly love me more than these?'
    'Yes, Lord,' he said, 'you know that I love you.'
    Jesus said, 'Feed my lambs.'

Again Jesus said, 'Simon son of John, do you truly love me?'

He answered, 'Yes, Lord, you know that I love you.'

Jesus said, 'Take care of my sheep.'

The third time he said to him, 'Simon son of John, do you love me?'

Peter was hurt because Jesus asked him the third time, 'Do you love me?' He said, 'Lord, you know all things; you know that I love you.'

Jesus said, 'Feed my sheep.'

(John 21:15–17)

Now that you have purified yourselves by obeying the truth so that you have sincere love for your brothers, love one another deeply, from the heart. For you have been born again, not of perishable seed, but of imperishable, through the living and enduring word of God.

(1 Peter 1:22,23)

Love is patient, love is kind. It does not envy, it does not boast, it is not proud. It is not rude, it is not self-seeking, it is not easily angered, it keeps no record of wrongs. Love does not delight in evil but rejoices with the truth. It always protects, always trusts, always hopes, always perseveres.

Love never fails.

(1 Corinthians 13:4–8)